Prisoners of the Past

Recognizing and Overcoming Post-Traumatic Stress Disorder

by

Harold Levine, D.O.

This book is not intended to replace personal medical care and/or professional supervision; there is no substitute for the experience and information that your doctor or mental health professional can provide. Rather, it is our hope that this book will provide additional information to help people understand the nature of post-traumatic stress disorder and its treatment.

Proper treatment should always be tailored to the individual. If you read something in this book that seems to conflict with your doctor or mental health professional's instructions, contact him/her. There may be sound reasons for recommending treatment that may differ from the information presented in this book.

If you have any questions about any treatment in this book, please consult your doctor or mental health care professional.

In addition, the names and cases used in this book do not represent actual people, but are composite cases drawn from several sources.

For information write:
Psychiatric Hospital Division of
National Medical Enterprises, Inc.
2700 Colorado Avenue
Santa Monica, California 90404

We gratefully acknowledge the following for permission to reprint previously published material:

The New York Times Company: Excerpts from "Ambushed by Memory, We Seek Refuge in Vain" by Lady Borton and "Even the Victim Can Be Slow to Recognize Rape" by Jane Gross. Copyright © 1988/91 by The New York Times Company. Reprinted by permission.

Woodbine House: Excerpt from *Vietnam Wives* by Virginia Matsakis, 1988. Reprinted with permission.

Other Books Available

___ **Get Smart About Weight Control** by Phillip M. Sinaikan, M.D. $6.95 0-929162-01-3
___ **Sixty Ways To Make Stress Work For You** by Andrew Slaby, M.D., Ph.D. $3.50 0-929162-02-1
___ **When Acting Out Isn't Acting** by Lynne W. Weisberg, M.D., Ph.D. and Rosalie Greenberg, M.D. $7.95 0-929162-03-X
___ **A Parent's Guide to Common and Uncommon School Problems** by David A. Gross, M.D. and Irl L. Extein, M.D. $8.95 0-929162-04-8
___ **High Times/Low Times: The Many Faces of Teenage Depression** by John E. Meeks, M.D. $8.95 0-929162-05-6
___ **Kids Out of Control** by Alan M. Cohen, M.D. $7.95 0-929162-06-4
___ **Guide to the New Medicines of the Mind** $8.95 0-929162-07-2
___ **Consumer's Guide to Psychiatric Diagnosis** by Mark A. Gould, M.D. $7.95 0-929162-08-0
___ **Light Up Your Blues: Understanding and Overcoming Seasonal Affective Disorders** by Robert N. Moreines, M.D. $8.95 0-929162-09-9
___ **On the Edge: The Love/Hate World of the Borderline Personality** by Neil D. Price, M.D. $7.95 0-929162-10-2
___ **Kids Who Do/Kids Who Don't: A Parent's Guide to Teens and Drugs** by Lorraine Henricks, M.D. $7.95 0-929162-11-0
___ **Psychiatric Skeletons: Tracing the Legacy of Mental Illness in the Family** by Steven Targum, M.D. $7.95 0-929162-12-9
___ **Life on a Roller Coaster: Coping with the Ups and Downs of Mood Disorders** by Ekkehard Othmer, M.D., Ph.D. and Sieglinde Othmer, Ph.D. $7.95 0-929162-13-7
___ **A Parent's Guide to Teens and Cults** by Larry E. Dumont, M.D. and Richard I. Altesman, M.D. $4.95 0-929162-14-5
___ **Family Addictions: A Guide for Surviving Drug and Alcohol Abuse** by Charles R. Norris, Jr., M.D. $9.99 0-929162-15-3
___ **No More Secrets/No More Shame: Understanding Sexual Abuse and Emotional Disorders** by David A. Sack, M.D. $7.95 0-929162-16-1
___ **The Family Contract: A Blueprint for Successful Parenting** by Howard I. Leftin, M.D. $9.99 0-929162-17-X
___ **Codependency, Sexuality and Depression** by William E. Thornton, M.D. $7.95 0-929162-18-8
___ **When Self-Help Isn't Enough: Overcoming Addiction and Psychiatric Disorders** by A. Scott Winter, M.D. $7.95 0-929162-19-6
___ **Divorce Recovery** by Allan J. Adler, M.D. and Christine Archambault $8.95 0-929162-21-8
___ **Kids on the Brink: Understanding the Teen Suicide Epidemic** by David B. Bergman, M.D. $7.95 0-929162-22-6
___ **A Woman's Guide to Mental Health** by Beryl W. Langley, M.D. and R. Joyce Stapp, M.D $8.95 0-929162-23-4
___ **Living With Pain** by William S. Makarowski, M.D. $8.95 0-929162-24-2
___ **Teens at Risk: How to Recognize and Prevent Adolescent Suicide** by Kevin Leehey, M.D. $8.95 0-929162-25-0
___ **The Joy of Parenting** by Bruce H. Axelrod, M.D $8.95 0-929162-27-7
___ **Living With Head Injury: A Guide For Families** by Richard C. Senelick, M.D. and Cathy E. Ryan $8.95 0-929162-28-5
___ **Caught in the Crossfire: The Impact of Divorce on Young People** by Lorraine Henricks, M.D. $8.95 0-929162-29-3
___ **Brain Storms: Recovery From Traumatic Brain Injury** by John W. Cassidy, M.D. $8.95 0-929162-39-0
___ **Los Detalles Sobre Las Drogas Y El Alcohol** by Mark Gold, M.D. $5.95 0-929162-40-4
___ **Sit Down and Pay Attention: Coping With Attention-Deficit Disorder Through the Life Cycle** by Ronald Goldberg, M.D. $9.99 0-929162-41-2
___ **Save the Males: Why Men are Mistreated, Misdiagnosed and Misunderstood** by Kenneth Wetcher, M.D., Art Barker and F. Rex McCaughtry $8.95 0-929162-42-0
___ **The Angry Child** by Kim J. Masters, M.D. $8.95 0-929162-49-8
___ **Fast Forwarding Through Childhood: Causes, Effects and Solutions for Stress in Children** by Mary F. Zesiewicz, M.D. $8.95 0-929162-50-1
___ **Prisoners of the Past: Recognizing and Overcoming Post-Traumatic Stress Disorder** by Harold Levine, D.O. $8.95 0-929162-51-X

1-800-874-2919

All prices subject to change without notice

To my father, Henry. His own pursuit of knowledge was my inspiration.

Acknowledgments

I wish to thank my teachers at the Menninger Foundation and my patients who have guided me toward searching for treatments when hope seems gone.

I would like to thank Al Smith, Brent Bryson, and Ron Bernstein for their support.

Many thanks to Marilyn Devroye for her invaluable contribution to this book.

Contents

Chapter One

Shell Shock: Variations on a Theme

KATHLEEN*, an experienced flight attendant for one of the major airlines, survived a plane crash that killed 51 people. The crash occurred two years ago, but Kathleen still isn't over the shock. Formerly a steady, dependable employee, she has recently taken a medical leave of absence for her "nerves." She suffers from nagging feelings of guilt, and her thoughts often turn to suicide.

CHUCK, a New York City patrolman, shot and killed a deranged man who was firing a semiautomatic rifle at a city bus. A court cleared him of all wrongdoing, but Chuck can't get the incident out of his mind. Flashbacks distract him. He's unable to concentrate. He drinks too much. He and his wife are getting a divorce.

RITA, a secretary who sometimes has to work late, was retrieving her car from a parking garage one evening when a stranger kidnaped her, drove her to an isolated spot, and

*Throughout this book, names and identities of people have been changed to preserve anonymity.

raped her at knifepoint. Rita has recovered physically, but she is now terrified of going outside alone. Her social life has shrunk to zero.

FRANK, who in 1991 served in Iraq during Operation Desert Storm, is safe at home now. He's enjoying real food again, sleeping between clean sheets, and making an effort to appreciate the companionship of his wife, Joan. But Frank is not the cheerful young man he was before the war. During the daylight hours, he's preoccupied and jumpy. At night, visions of the mangled, disfigured bodies of Iraqi soldiers invade his dreams. Several nights a week, Frank wakes up screaming.

• • •

What Kathleen, Chuck, Rita, and Frank have in common is *post-traumatic stress disorder*, or PTSD—a psychiatric condition that develops in some (but not all) people who live through a severe trauma.

What dos PTSD do to people? Basically, it prevents them from getting over the trauma and returning to their ordinary, everyday lives.

- Some people with PTSD keep on reliving the trauma they experienced; they have actual *flashbacks* to the traumatic moment.
- Others act *numb*, withdrawing from family and friends and refusing to meet new people.
- Some turn to *alcohol and drugs, reckless driving*, or *high-stakes gambling* to try to "feel alive" again.
- Others become *irritable* or even *violent*—lashing out at people on the job, or abusing their spouse or children.
- Many suffer from frequent, excruciating *headaches*, or from bodily pains for which doctors can find no physical cause.
- Many have *nightmares* and struggle with *insomnia*.

As you'll see in the pages that follow, PTSD isn't a new phenomenon. Since human history is punctuated by natural disasters and wars, PTSD is probably as old as humanity itself.

But although it's nothing new, PTSD has been making the news more and more often in recent years. Does that mean life is more traumatic now than in the past? Not necessarily. To my mind, PTSD is now a "high-profile" problem because it has become a *treatable* condition.

No longer do victims of PTSD have to suffer their guilt, pain, and anxiety in lonely silence. The right combination of physical and psychological therapy can help them overcome the delayed effects of trauma and get back to the satisfying life they want to live.

But for PTSD victims to benefit from treatment, they first need to know that help is available. That's partly why I've written this book: to tell people what PTSD is, how it can affect survivors of severe trauma, and how professional treatment can help relieve it.

The other reason I've written this book is to put in a good word for prevention. Most people still don't realize that it's best to treat PTSD before it actually develops—by giving *immediate* counseling to accident and trauma victims. I hope this book will convince you that post-trauma counseling is not "coddling," but true preventive medicine.

WHAT COUNTS AS POST-TRAUMATIC STRESS DISORDER?

According to *DSM-III-R*, the diagnostic manual that's often called the "psychiatrist's bible," people with post-traumatic stress disorder share these five basic characteristics:

1. They have survived *severe* trauma or distress. The manual refers to this as "an event that is outside the range of usual human experience," such as a serious threat to one's life or physical integrity; a serious threat or harm to one's children, spouse, or friends; destruction of one's home or community; or seeing someone get seriously injured or killed.

2. They regularly *reexperience* the trauma in some disturbing way. Their "flashbacks" might be recurrent memories . . . or nightmares . . . or weirdly realistic you-are-there feelings . . . or intense fear triggered by "reminder" sights and sounds.

3. They *avoid* thinking about the trauma. Perhaps they block out the thoughts and feelings they had during the trauma, or steer clear of situations that remind them of the trauma, or actually forget all or part of the trauma episode (this last is a symptom called "psychogenic amnesia").

Or they become *withdrawn and uncommunicative.* Perhaps they feel remote and detached from other people, or expect that they won't live long, or "forget" how to feel and act lovingly. Young children with PTSD may forget their toilet training, or revert to baby talk.

4. Their *nervous system goes on "hyper-alert"* in some way. Perhaps they sleep poorly, or have violent outbursts of temper, or can't concentrate on anything. Or they may be constantly keyed up, edgy, and easily startled. A person who survived a plane crash might start to feel sweaty and panicky upon boarding a plane.

5. Their symptoms (as described in 2,3, and 4) last for *a month or more.* If the symptoms did not appear until six months or more after the traumatic event, doctors call the condition *delayed-onset PTSD.*

OLD-TIMERS CALLED IT SHELL SHOCK

People familiar with the military have always known about PTSD, but they've had different names for it. A colleague of mine told the following story about his great-uncle Harry:

Harry, who was a teenager at the start of World War I, managed to enlist in the army at the age of 17. He served in the trenches in France, saw a great deal of suffering, and came home with what was then called *shell shock*. According to his wife, Harry had periodic bad dreams from which he would awaken crying inconsolably.

Harry eventually outgrew the worst of his shell shock, but some of the dread stayed with him for life. At one point, during his retirement years, he won a prize in a nationally advertised sweepstakes. His prize turned out to be a week-long trip for two, all expenses paid, to Paris. To everyone's amazement, and his wife's dismay, Harry decided to forfeit the prize. With great firmness he explained, "I've seen enough of France to last me a lifetime."

My colleague said that at the time, he and his relatives all thought Uncle Harry was just being stubborn and silly. But in hindsight, he realizes that his great-uncle was showing *avoidant* behavior—one of the symptoms of PTSD—50 years after the fact. His severe trauma as a doughboy had left him psychologically scarred for life.

Shell shock isn't the only old-time name for PTSD. Some military doctors, seeing extreme emotional upset in war-weary soldiers and former prisoners of war, called this syndrome *battle fatigue*. And in 1921, Sigmund Freud wrote about the condition using the term *war neurosis*.

The Vietnam war, of course, left many American soldiers and sailors emotionally crippled. Newspaper and magazine articles, books, television documentaries, and medical studies all hammered home the reality of "Vietnam syndrome." But not until 1980 did the American Psychiatric Association classify "Vietnam syndrome" and other combat-related conditions under the general heading of post-traumatic stress disorder.

DISASTERS, ACCIDENTS, AND CATASTROPHES

Gradually, doctors realized that horrendous combat and prisoner-of-war experiences weren't the only possible causes of PTSD. *Natural disasters* such as tornadoes, tidal waves, and earthquakes could be just as devastating. In October of 1989, a week after a California earthquake that measured 7.1 on the Richter scale, the *San Francisco Chronicle* polled Bay Area residents and found that three out of five were having emotional difficulties. As one news article put it, "Their homes may be sound but their sleep is unsettled. The sound of a siren, whatever its purpose, sets nerves to jangling. A drive over a bridge is an occasion for fear."* Not all of these people went on to develop PTSD, but some did.

Accidents and catastrophes can also trigger PTSD. Five months after an Avianca jetliner crashed on Long Island, New York, in 1990, killing 73 passengers, some survivors reported that they often relived the crash in nightmares. "There are moments when I wake up and I'm crying," said a woman whose four-month-old son died in the crash. + Another survivor said the possibility of her own death was always on her mind. She had become careless about spending: "I say, 'What the hell. I'll buy it now because I may be dead tomorrow.' But later I feel guilty. It's a mental confusion."**

RAPE AND RANDOM VIOLENCE

Another possible trigger of PTSD is *sexual assault*, by either a stranger or an acquaintance. Doctors and lay people are

---

* Gross, Jane, "Aftershocks Damaging Frail Psyches," *New York Times*, October 26, 1989, p. B-8.

\+ Navarro, Mireya, "For Some, No Escape From L.I. Jet Crash," *New York Times*, June 25, 1990, p. B-1.

** Ibid.

beginning to understand that "date rape"—forced intercourse with an acquaintance—can be as traumatic as rape by a total stranger. According to a report in the *New York Times*, one woman, who had been dating a particular man for several months before he raped her on New Year's Eve, was so traumatized afterward that she moved out of town, changed jobs five times within six years, and put on fifty pounds.* Other date-rape victims went through months or years of self-doubt, guilt, nightmares, bulimia, and other emotional problems before they sought counseling.

Random violence is yet another potential PTSD trigger. As you saw earlier, the official definition of post-traumatic stress disorder specifies that the traumatic trigger event must be "outside the range of ordinary human experience." In fact, though, the residents of some violence-torn urban areas routinely endure exposure to shootings, stabbings, and muggings. For these unfortunate people, instances of traumatic stress fall *within* the range of everyday experience.

For instance, a 1991 study of Detroit residents aged 21 to 30 reported that fully 40 percent of them had had exposure to an official "PTSD stressor"—sudden injury or serious accident, physical assault or rape, seeing someone seriously hurt or killed, or hearing of the sudden death of a close relative or friend. + Nine percent developed PTSD.

HEART ATTACK

Even *serious illness* may set PTSD in motion. Hospital psychiatrists have described how PTSD can develop in the

* Gross, Jane, "Even the Victim Can Be Slow to Recognize Rape," *New York Times*, May 28, 1991, p. A14.

+ Bower, B., "Trauma Disorder Strikes Many Young Adults," *Science News*, 139:13 (March 30, 1991), p. 198.

wake of a heart attack.* One published report describes a man whose heart attack seemed to have changed his personality completely. Family members said that when this man came home from the hospital, he seemed strangely detached and disinterested. He startled easily, and often lashed out at the son he had formerly cherished. Although his doctors told him he could resume normal activities, he never took more than a few steps at a time, and he refused to venture outside the house. Soon after falling asleep at night he would awaken, clutch his wife, and scream that he was falling into a black hole. It developed that his behavior was a form of PTSD.

ONLOOKERS, FAMILIES, AND FRIENDS MAY SUFFER, TOO

All too commonly, books about PTSD focus on only the direct victims of crimes, accidents, and disasters, but say nothing about the people close to them. I'd like to correct that by noting that the family members and friends of trauma victims are also vulnerable to PTSD—as are rescue workers, and even bystanders who happen to witness disasters and violent crimes:

- A fire swept through a London Underground station in 1987, killing 31 people and severely burning seven more. In the aftermath, *680 people* eventually accepted psychiatric treatment. Included in that number, besides survivors of the fire, were bystanders, hospital personnel, ambulance workers, police officers, and firefighters.**

---

* Kutz, Ilan, et al: "Post-Traumatic Stress Disorder Following Myocardial Infarction," *General Hospital Psychiatry* 10, 1988, p. 169-176.

** Psychiatric Intervention After Disaster," *Lancet*, July 15, 1989, p. 138.

- A national survey found that more than 4 million American adults are *indirect* victims of homicide—that is, surviving relatives of those who died. Some 250,000 of them are currently suffering from PTSD, as long as ten years after the crime.*
- An elderly woman whose adult daughter and baby granddaughter died at the hand of a knife-wielding, drug-crazed attacker, said, "It's been five years now since it happened, but it still seems like yesterday. In some ways, as time passes, it gets even harder to live with."

Unfortunately, many indirect victims of a traumatic event strenuously resist offers of counseling, even if they are suffering from serious PTSD. They tend to think that because they weren't really part of the action, they shouldn't need treatment or don't deserve it. Yet they do need attention: After all, they are the ones who will provide much of the support to the primary victims of the trauma. Thus, after a major disaster, a priority issue for those in charge is finding all the people who were potentially traumatized, and making them a direct offer of psychiatric treatment.

WHY NOT EVERYONE?

Already you may be wondering: In the wake of a severe traumas, why do only *some* people suffer from PTSD? Are certain people at special risk?

In one sense, yes. Through the years, I've found that the people most likely to succumb to PTSD after a catastrophe

* Raymond, Chris Anne, "Study Says Memories of Violent Death Linger in Survivors, Trigger Psychosocial Problems." *JAMA* 259:24, June 24, 1988, p. 3524.

are those who are emotionally vulnerable to start with. The best way to explain this is through a simple example:

Let's say two people, Martha and Rochelle, are both riding a crowded train.

- **Martha** is happily married, has two healthy children, and is on her way to visit her sister, with whom she gets along well. Her basic outlook on life is serene and confident.
- **Rochelle** recently went through a bitter divorce, is unemployed, has few marketable job skills, and is no longer on speaking terms with her parents. Her basic outlook on life is bitter and distrustful.

Suddenly, disaster strikes. Through a switching error, the train derails, and the car in which Martha and Rochelle are riding overturns. Screams fill the air. The train is reduced to twisted metal and broken glass. A dozen people die. Martha and Rochelle suffer broken bones and lacerations, but both survive.

Six months later, Martha has recovered, emotionally as well as physically. She has scars from her injuries, but she knows they will fade in time. She went through a period of hesitancy about ever riding a train again, but she has purposely taken several train trips to prove to herself that she can do it. Although she still has vivid memories of the tragedy, they don't prevent her from living her ordinary life.

But Rochelle, whose physical injuries were actually less serious than Martha's, suffers from PTSD. Her nightmares of the train crash are so frequent that insomnia has become a serious problem for her. She shuns contact with friends, and has become severely withdrawn. She knows she should get a job, but she can't motivate herself to look for work. Her life has ground almost to a halt. She needs psychiatric help.

Why did PTSD strike Rochelle and not Martha? The reason is that Rochelle was more emotionally vulnerable at the time of the accident. She lacked self-confidence. She had few social supports. Her life looked bleak. She was in worse shape than Martha when the accident occurred, and she had inadequate support afterward. For Rochelle, the train wreck was the straw that broke the camel's back.

SCOPE OF THE TRAUMA

In another sense, though, it's impossible to predict who will and who will not suffer from PTSD after a catastrophe. Much depends on the scope and duration of the trauma.

For instance, to take an example from World War II, I think it's fair to say that *everyone* who survived Hitler's concentration camps suffered from PTSD to a greater or lesser extent. Horror and deprivation on that scale are guaranteed to affect everyone involved. Afterward, for a given individual, the crucial question is *how long the symptoms will last*. Again, though, it's reasonable to assume that given equal exposure to trauma, the person who was initially stable and confident will probably recover normal functioning sooner than the person who was initially unstable, insecure, or depressed.

Now that you know what this book is about, I'd like to tell you in more detail about the various symptoms of PTSD. Let's move ahead.

CHAPTER TWO

KNOCKED FOR A LOOP

What does it feel like to be the victim of post-traumatic stress disorder? How do people with PTSD act toward others? To fill in the picture, this chapter will give you descriptions of three people suffering from PTSD. Their traumas were different. But in significant ways, their reactions were similar. All of them encountered disaster severe enough to knock them for a loop.

A LEGACY OF INCEST

Jean, as described in *The Shattered Self,** is a 36-year-old woman who lived through a violence-wracked childhood. Her mother, cold and distant with her three children, once stabbed Jean's father in the eye and blinded him.

After Jean's parents divorced, her mother married a man who ran the household as if it were a concentration camp. This stepfather, whom Jean feared intensely and obeyed

* Ulman, Richard B., and Brothers, Doris, *The Shattered Self*. Hillside, N.J.: The Analytic Press, 1988.

automatically, first raped her when she was 12. Soon after that, the stepfather turned their home into what Jean called "a little whorehouse," forcing sex on Jean and her two sisters while their mother, sleeping on a couch in the living room, remained apparently unaware.

Jean reacted to these ongoing sexual assaults by pretending they weren't really happening. She took pride in her ability to look and act completely neutral while her stepfather raped her.

Her monumental effort at self-control spilled over into her daydreams: She had frequent, prolonged visions of someone tying her up and torturing her while she took care never to show her pain or fear.

When Jean was 15, her mother shot herself in the stomach in a suicide attempt. Jean felt abandoned and betrayed. Up till then, she had assumed that she and her mother would always be together, no matter how miserable their existence; the suicide attempt convinced her that her mother did not share that loyalty. After her mother came home from the hospital, Jean felt herself living on the edge of insanity. She suffered from vertigo, and had numerous bizarre premonitions.

Jean went to college and earned a bachelor's degree in criminology, but then drifted aimlessly, supporting herself by dealing drugs and occasionally prostituting herself. In her sexual relationships she opted to play the masochist, submitting to whippings and beatings in a detached, dazed state of mind. Afterward, her memories of the beatings were vague. Only the marks on her body proved to her that she had actually suffered.

Periodically Jean would "go into isolation": After laying in a supply of food, and phoning to tell people she would be out of town, she would spend several days in bed, sleeping, resting, and occasionally drawing. She became hooked on marijuana and amphetamines. She was chronically hyperalert, startled easily, and had trouble sleeping. When she finally sought therapy, the diagnosis for her condition was PTSD.

STABBED AND LEFT FOR DEAD

Guy, a lanky Californian in his mid-40s, had reason to distrust life. His universe had first fallen apart when he was only 7 years old. On a day that Guy still remembers, his father came home, realized his wife was in bed with another man, kicked in the bedroom door, and shot both of them dead. The police arrived, arrested the father, and took him away. Guy and his brother, cowering in the dining room, didn't actually witness the murder, but they understood what had happened. Their innocent childhood trust had exploded in the gunfire.

The two brothers grew up in a foster home. Guy slid through high school, staying out of trouble, but making no close friends of either sex. He tried college for a while, then dropped out. For the next twenty-five years he supported himself by doing odd jobs: courier work and house painting, but mainly carpentry. He remained unmarried. People considered him slightly distant, but pleasant.

During an economic recession, Guy lost his carpentry job and fell on hard times. He was ineligible for unemployment benefits, and he did not even consider applying for welfare. Instead, he arranged to live at the home of married friends until he got back on his feet.

Outwardly, the friends appeared to be an ordinary couple. But Guy quickly discovered that their relationship was abusive, and he grew increasingly uneasy living with them. At one point, the friend argued violently with his wife, then pulled out a revolver, aimed it at Guy, and threatened him. Guy was badly shaken. That evening, instead of driving back to their house to sleep, he pulled his car off the highway and onto a cliff by the ocean, intending to camp there for the night.

At about two A.M. Guy awoke to the crash of shattering glass. Four thugs, one wielding a baseball bat and another carrying a knife, had broken into his car. They hit him over the head with the bat, grabbed his wallet, stabbed him in the chest and stomach, and left him for dead.

Fortunately, someone dragged Guy to a hospital, and three weeks later he was well enough to be released. Although Guy was healing physically, his personality seemed radically changed. At night, recurrent nightmares of the attack kept him awake. By day, he had no energy, continued to lose weight, and avoided people he knew. He seemed paralyzed, unable to look for a job or a place to live, uninterested even in carrying on a normal conversation. He was a hollow shell of his former self.

Eventually, a therapist arranged for Guy to enter a psychiatric hospital. The diagnosis: PTSD.

A WOMAN IN THE KILLING FIELDS

Journalists have written reams about male veterans who suffer from "post-Vietnam syndrome." Relatively few, however, have bothered to find out how military *women*—mainly nurses—fared in the Vietnam war and its aftermath.

Ruth, as described in *A Woman's Recovery from the Trauma of War,** is a 39-year-old who served as a Navy nurse in Vietnam in 1969 and 1970. The bright, dutiful daughter of devout Catholic parents, she graduated at the top of her class, and lived at home until she went on active military duty at the age of 23.

* Rothblum, Esther D., and Cole, Ellen, eds., *A Woman's Recovery From the Trauma of War*. New York: Haworth Press, 1986.

In her first year of service Ruth worked in New York, treating troops who had been badly wounded in the 1968 Tet offensive. She routinely cared for men suffering from horrible burns, severed limbs, and severe infections.

Then the Navy sent her on a nine-month tour of duty at a military hospital in Da Nang. Help and equipment were in short supply, and the hospital was the target of continual mortar shelling, sniper fire, and grenade attacks.

It's difficult even to describe the daily horror of Ruth's tour of duty in Vietnam. The patients she saw were in desperate shape, with whole-body burns, arms and legs blown off, or final-stage malaria. She never had the opportunity to nurse even a single person back to wellness; her patients either died or were evacuated. Once, while Ruth was off duty and having lunch at a riverside cafe, she looked out over the water just as the bodies of three drowned airmen bobbed to the surface. She and her medical colleagues made it a point never to discuss their emotions about the death and dying that surrounded them. To maintain a brave facade, they drank heavily.

Back in the U.S., Ruth, who did not realize that she had contracted tuberculosis in Vietnam, began to complain of chronic pain, chills, and fever. Various therapists, thinking her trouble was psychosomatic, tried to treat her for emotional distress; it was two years before a doctor made the correct diagnosis. Meanwhile, to dull the physical pain, Ruth drank. She stopped seeing her former friends, and grew distant from her family. She entered graduate school, dropped out, and then drifted from one low-paying job to another. Even after getting treatment for her tuberculosis, Ruth kept drinking heavily.

Ten years after her return from Vietnam, Ruth finally admitted that she needed professional help. She was drinking more than ever, and feeling worse. She often had hallucinations of dead and maimed bodies. Sometimes she imagined she smelled infected flesh. The sound of a helicopter gave her flashbacks—frighteningly realistic episodes in which she felt she was back in Vietnam and under attack. Terrifying dreams prevented her from getting a full night's sleep; she often dreamed that one of the badly wounded men she had cared for was pursuing her, determined to kill her in revenge for his suffering. She often had trouble thinking and remembering. At times, anxiety made it hard for her to speak; at other times she felt strangely numb inside. Ruth was extremely unsure of herself, and even told the therapist she thought she might be exaggerating some of her symptoms "to get attention."

But Ruth wasn't exaggerating anything. Without a doubt, she was suffering from PTSD.

PRISONERS OF THE PAST

As you can see, these three people experienced radically different kinds of trauma:

- Jean endured years of callous treatment and incestuous assaults; the combined weight of these multiple traumas gradually warped her sense of herself and eroded her ability to cope.
- Guy suffered a devastating childhood trauma, seemed reasonably stable as an adult, but then fell apart in the wake of a five-minute episode of gratuitous brutality.
- Ruth came from a stable family background, but then lived through two intense years of wartime horror that sent her "over the edge."

Yet all three shared certain symptoms—the symptoms of PTSD. They *reexperienced* their trauma at unexpected moments. They suffered from *insomnia and nightmares*. They acted *numb and unresponsive* toward other people, either constantly or sporadically. They *avoided* activities and situations that called up memories of past trauma. And they *startled easily*.

That's the overall picture of PTSD. You still may find it puzzling that such different experiences could lead to the development of the same psychiatric syndrome. So in the next chapter, I'll focus on the nuts and bolts of PTSD—how the troublesome symptoms develop, and, just as important, why.

Chapter Three

Genesis of a Nightmare

Trauma. The very word is ominous, conjuring up images of car or plane wreckage, bleeding wounds, a sexual assault, or the sight of a lifeless body.

No matter what the trauma, those who survive it—whether or not they develop post-traumatic stress disorder—pass through certain predictable emotional and mental stages: denial, anger, blame, shame, guilt, fear, intellectualization, hostility, and unresolved conflicts. Looking at that list, you might suppose that one stage plays itself out and then neatly gives way to the next stage. Since human beings are such complicated creatures, however, that's not how it happens. In real life, the stages overlap and also loop back on one another.

For example, Rod, a solidly-built teenager, survived a motorcycle accident but lost a leg in the process. Immediately following the amputation, Rod seemed matter-of-fact about it, acting as if it were no big deal. Sure enough, this was *denial*, the first stage of reaction to a trauma. When the first visitors showed up at his hospital bedside, Rod welcomed them gratefully and told them he was glad just to be alive. Anxious to show that he was in control of himself and the situation, he had leaped ahead to the stage of *intellectualization*. But as his wounds healed, and he realized fully how the amputation would forever change his lifestyle, his good-natured acceptance changed to surliness and then fury: He had backtracked to the stage of *anger*. To the casual observer, it seemed that Rod was veering off in the wrong direction. But that wasn't so. Unpleasant and uncomfortable as it was for everyone else, furious anger was a normal, necessary part of Rod's recovery from a severe trauma.

Returning to the issue of PTSD, let's take a look at how PTSD symptoms can develop—focusing in turn on each of the stages of reaction to trauma, and paying attention to how each state *feels* to the survivor.

DENIAL: FIRST LINE OF DEFENSE

Usually denial is the first and shortest stage, lasting for only about the first 24 hours after disaster strikes. Denial is a protective mechanism, a trick that the mind plays on itself to shut out the overwhelming stress of a catastrophe. It's valuable as a temporary measure, because it keeps traumatized people from "falling apart" before they can reach help.

Denial, in fact, is the explanation for why so many victims of rape don't report the rape right away. The truth is, they don't immediately *acknowledge* that what happened to them was rape.

A *New York Times* article on "acquaintance rape" described one woman's very typical reaction to rape:

> She figured she had made a stupid mistake by agreeing to drive a fellow student home from a party. She wondered if she had led him on by going into his house.
>
> She asked herself if she could have fought back more vigorously when he threw her to the bed and forced her

to have sexual intercourse. And when the attack was over, she felt embarrassed rather than angry and apologized for 'not wanting sex.'

"I put the burden on myself," this woman explained, many years later. "I thought it was all my fault."*

But denial, when it persists well past the immediate danger period, is counterproductive and can foster the development of PTSD. For some "acquaintance rape" victims, the denial stage goes on for years. Troublesome *chronic* symptoms emerge—bulimia, self-doubt, guilt, anxiety, irrational fears, nightmares, flashbacks to the rape, emotional numbness. Until these victims get competent counseling, they don't realize that the root cause of their symptoms is the raw, unprocessed trauma of rape.

People who set up very high walls of denial may not develop PTSD until months, or even many years, after their trauma. A well-known example from medical literature is a Boston woman who survived the Coconut Grove nightclub fire of 1942, in which 492 people died. This woman first began having symptoms of PTSD almost forty years after the fire.

ANGER: PUTTING NERVOUS ENERGY TO WORK

Late one afternoon, as Patti and Joe were unloading groceries from the back of their station wagon, they waved to a neighbor woman who was just arriving home from work. A minute later this same woman dashed out the front door of her house, screaming at them to come and "help Duane, help Duane." They dropped the groceries and dashed to her

* Gross, Jane, "Even the Victim Can Be Slow to Recognize Rape," *New York Times*, May 28, 1991, p. A14.

aid. But when they burst into her front hallway, it was far too late: Duane, her 40-year-old son, was swinging from a rope tied to the top of the stair rail.

In a panic, Joe ran for a knife to cut the rope, while Patti rushed to the telephone to call the police. Minutes later, rescue workers arrived. When they saw that Duane had been dead for hours and that there was no hope of resuscitating him, they bundled him onto a stretcher, covered him with a sheet, and took him to the hospital to be pronounced dead.

Patti's reaction to the rescue workers was pure, deep anger. "Those bastards!" she shouted, as neighbors emerged from their houses to see what the commotion was all about. "Those lousy bastards! They're too chicken to give him mouth-to-mouth resuscitation. Those cowards! They're all afraid of getting AIDS!"

There wasn't any rational reason for Patti's anger. Duane had hanged himself early in the day, and his body was already stiff. The rescue workers were not cowards. Mouth-to-mouth resuscitation was a lost cause, and Patti, who was a nurse, knew this. Yet her horror over Duane's suicide had reached the bursting point. Her tremendous charge of nervous energy released itself in a blind fury. She lashed out at the nearest target—the rescue squad. Hours afterward, she was still complaining bitterly about the rescue workers and their cowardice.

Trauma-related high energy, the fight-or-flight reaction, develops when the body pumps out a tremendous shot of the stress hormone adrenaline. A burst of adrenaline is an appropriate physical response to a life-threatening situation. In PTSD, however, the body keeps on firing inappropriate salvos of adrenaline, months or even years after the crisis has passed. These are the possible results:

- A hair-trigger startle reflex
- Extreme irritability

- Violent outbursts of temper
- A keyed-up, paranoid state known as hypervigilance

If it becomes *chronic,* any one of these states of unusual nervous arousal can by a symptom of PTSD.

BLAME: WHOSE FAULT IS THIS, ANYWAY?

After a trauma, blame can turn either outward toward others, or inward toward the self.

Barbara hurried her two little daughters into the car but didn't bother fastening their seat belts. She was running late, and besides, the swim club was less than a mile away. She drove to the end of her street, perfunctorily glancing both ways as she leaned into the left turn. The teenage driver, high on cocaine, had run a red light; he was doing sixty miles an hour when he broadsided Barbara's car. Barbara emerged from the accident with broken legs and a crushed pelvis. Both daughters survived, too, but with permanent brain damage.

A year and a half after the accident, Barbara's husband, Tom, formerly a cheerful, optimistic fellow, was consumed with thoughts of revenge. For the 18-year-old monster who had destroyed his daughters' future, he wanted the electric chair or, at the very least, life imprisonment without parole. He spent his evenings at the law library, doing "research" that he thought would help his attorney. Barbara, still somewhat handicapped from her injuries, badly needed Tom's help and support with the care of the wheelchair-bound girls. But Tom, bitter and restless, focused all his emotional energy on the legal case. He barely noticed his daughters' needs or his wife's distress. His will to fix the blame had become an obsession.

At the opposite extreme was Amanda, whose alcoholic

husband stormed out of the house one night to escape her bitter accusations. He was already blind drunk, and as he lurched toward yet another bar he stumbled into the path of an oncoming car. The impact killed him instantly. Amanda, stunned by her husband's death, placed the blame squarely on herself. If she hadn't screamed at him to get out of the house, she thought, he would still be alive. Eighteen months after the tragedy, more depressed and disturbed than ever, she quit her job. She had no self-confidence, and felt she didn't deserve to live.

Tom's impulse to blame turned outward, Amanda's turned inward. Either way, for certain people who suffer from PTSD, a *chronic* focus on blame can make clear thinking difficult or impossible.

SHAME AND GUILT: WHEN VICTIMS PUT THEMSELVES DOWN

A deep sense of shame is particularly likely to afflict victims of rape. This is because of a cultural assumption that's very common, though largely unacknowledged: the assumption that, in some way, a woman who was raped must have been asking for it.

Of course, such an assumption is highly unfair to women. Judges, jurors, or even witnesses who think this way can't help seeing rape through a warped lens. They are apt to decide that virtually *anything* a woman said or did before the rape constituted "provocative" behavior. Did the woman speak to the man in a friendly way? That was provocative. Was she wearing attractive clothes? That was provocative. Was she out by herself at night? That was provocative.

Men aren't the only ones to make the damaging assumption that women who get raped were asking for it. Women believe this, too. Many women who are recovering from rape ask themselves, How could I have allowed this to happen to me?

If their shame becomes *chronic* it not only kills their sexual desire, but causes them to withdraw socially. Inappropriate feelings of shame often contribute to the avoidant behavior that so often characterizes PTSD.

What about guilt? "Survivor guilt," a term you may have heard, often afflicts people who walk away from a catastrophe in which others perished. These people wonder, Why did I live through this disaster, while that three-year-old child died? They think perhaps they *should* have died. They fear they saved their own skins at other people's expense—for example, by running out of a burning building instead of helping everyone else escape.

In PTSD, survivor guilt becomes *chronic* and corrosive. Like shame, guilt can cause survivors of trauma to enclose themselves in a psychological shell. To escape what they imagine to be disapproval and scorn, they withdraw from the world, walling themselves off from contact with family and friends.

FEAR: THE DELAYED REACTION

Somewhat surprisingly, people who act like heroes throughout a catastrophe usually feel no fear at the time. If there's fear, it occurs beforehand—for instance, when the plane engine suddenly bursts into flames, or when the evil-looking stranger suddenly steps out of the shadows. At the point when the plane crash-lands, or the stranger brandishes a gun and demands cash, the victims' stress hormones take charge, allowing them to act. Temporarily, at least, there's no time for fear.

But fear may develop afterward. Eileen, whose car was rear-ended by a tractor-trailer on a crowded highway, was a nervous driver for several months after her accident. Fred, who capsized in a choppy lake and almost drowned in the icy water, was fearful of sailing for the rest of the season.

In people with PTSD, *chronic* fear lurks just beneath the surface of everyday life, provoking nightmares, flashbacks, and bizarre behavior. Yolanda, whose PTSD developed after she was mugged, could sleep at night only if she braced her feet against the door; that way, she said, no one could enter her room without waking her. Dan, a Vietnam veteran with PTSD, could not bear for his wife to hold his hand in the supermarket because it interfered with his sense of "combat readiness."

Some people with PTSD actively seek situations that remind them of their trauma. Janelle, whose father had sexually abused her throughout her childhood, became a prostitute. Xuan, who fled from a terrorist regime in Southeast Asia, later became a mercenary soldier. Usually, people like this are desperately trying to master their chronic fear, rather than let their fear master them.

INTELLECTUALIZATION: WHO'S IN CHARGE HERE?

People need to feel that they understand, and at least partly control, the things that happen to them. There's a reason why trauma tends to do heavy psychological damage: It undermines the victims' sense that they understand life and can control their surroundings.

People who are recovering from a traumatic experience often turn to religion or philosophy to explain what happened to them. They intellectualize in order to make sense of the trauma, put it in perspective, and recover their sense that they are in charge of their lives. A man who was rescued from a plane crash may get past his "survivor guilt" by accepting that God wanted him to live. A woman who saw police officers turn a convenience store robbery into a fatal shootout may tell herself that the criminals got what they deserved.

In people with PTSD, however, the process of intellectualization has aborted. These people see no satisfactory explanation for the trauma they experienced. Their former assumptions about safety, trust, and human dignity now strike them as naive. They are *chronically* at the mercy of their fears and doubts.

Charlene survived a brutal sexual assault. She reported the incident, but the local police were indifferent and unhelpful. The world began to seem like a strange and hostile place. "Before this happened," she said, "I always thought life was basically good. And I thought the police were there to help people. Now I know better." Charlene suffers from nightmares, flashbacks, and emotional numbness—classic symptoms of PTSD.

One theory holds that traumatic experiences occur on a continuum of acceptability:

- Traumas on the "fairly understandable" end of the scale are events for which no one is to blame, such as tornadoes, floods, and earthquakes.
- Traumas in the "possibly understandable" middle portion of the scale are disasters caused by human error, such as drunk-driving accidents.
- Traumas on the "totally unacceptable" end of the scale are acts of deliberate cruelty, such as rape, violent crime, or torture.

According to this theory, the less "acceptable" the trauma, the greater the risk that the victim will develop PTSD, and the more serious the PTSD symptoms will be.

HOSTILITY: GET THE HELL OUT OF HERE

Bob's wife, Jessie, had been very depressed for more than a year. She was seeing a therapist, but the results weren't impressive. One day, Jessie took a large overdose of sleeping pills. When Bob came home from work and found her in a coma, he called for an ambulance. Jessie went directly into intensive care, but it was already too late: She died several hours later. In his initial shock, Bob was extremely hostile to the doctors and nurses who had treated Jessie. He shouted, screamed, threatened a malpractice suit. Eventually, though, he collapsed in sobs of grief, and his hostility drained away.

In people with PTSD, however, hostility may become *chronic*. Francine, who had been sexually abused as a child, mistrusted most men, but she was attracted to Raymond and she told herself he was special. One night, she and Raymond went out dancing and drinking—and the evening ended in rape. After that, Francine's attitude toward men hardened. "I only date rich guys," she said. "I make them spend a lot of money on me. And as soon as a guy starts acting like he's in love with me, I treat him like dirt."

Jeff, a Vietnam veteran who lives in self-imposed isolation, is prone to fits of violent anger. "I rip out doors and bust up furniture when I'm mad," he said. "I moved out here to get away from people. I was afraid I'd hurt somebody."

UNFINISHED BUSINESS: INTRUSIONS AND AVOIDANCES

Trauma, especially if it involves sudden death, leaves the survivors mulling over things they wish they had or hadn't said or done to the deceased. In time, most of these survivors makes peace with themselves, realizing that such ruminating helps neither themselves nor those who died.

In PTSD, however, unfinished business related to the trauma becomes *chronic*, taking on a life of its own. The unresolved issues may *intrude* at unexpected moments, causing insomnia, nightmares, disturbing daydreams, and flashbacks to the trauma. Or the festering emotional issues may simmer beneath the surface, causing the person to feel emotionally numb—and to *avoid* people, activities, or thoughts that might "stir the pot." Either way, the symptoms interfere with normal, everyday functioning. Many people who suffer from PTSD have both intrusive *and* avoidant symptoms.

AN OVERSTIMULATED NERVOUS SYSTEM

PTSD shows up as a set of psychological symptoms, but doctors are aware—and you should be aware, too—that it's also a *physical* condition.

Scientist initially discovered that people with PTSD pump out far too much adrenaline, the "fight-or-flight" hormone. A more recent discovery is that people with PTSD also pump out excessive amounts of two important brain chemicals, *dopamine* and *serotonin*, which also stimulate the nervous system. Together, these three body chemicals cause the "hot" symptoms we've discussed—symptoms such as insomnia, nightmares, jumpiness, and extreme irritability.

But over the long haul, the body can't tolerate all that extra stimulation of the nervous system. To try to tone things down, it pumps out other complex organic chemicals, *cortisol* and *acetylcholine*. These put the brakes on the nervous system, all right, but they can cause problems, too. Too much of them causes the "cool" symptoms that are also characteristic of PTSD—symptoms such as depression, lack of motivation, emotional numbness, and avoidance of people and normal activities.

Thus, the symptoms of PTSD start out like normal, predictable reactions to extreme stress, but then become *chronic*. From what we understand so far, the biochemistry of PTSD is that of an overexcited nervous system, with the body desperately, but inefficiently, trying to calm the system down:

1. First, a traumatic experience *revs up* the nervous system—and leaves it in high gear.
2. When the madly racing nervous system spins out of control, the body tries to *slam on the brakes*—but the engine is still revving very fast.
3. The power system and the braking system vie for dominance. "Speedup" nervous symptoms (nightmares, flashbacks) alternate with "slowdown" nervous symptoms (numbness, withdrawal), causing a *bumpy ride*. The person feels confused, uncomfortable, and eventually exhausted and desperate.

Recovering from PTSD, as you've probably begun to suspect, is a process of resetting the nervous system to a comfortable cruising speed. But I'm getting a little ahead of myself. The next chapter, which focuses on *diagnosis*, will show you how a doctor decides whether a patient is actually suffering from PTSD—or from something else.

Chapter Four

Going by the Book

How does a doctor decide whether a person has post-traumatic stress disorder, or something else? It's not always as easy as it might seem!

But wait, you might say—diagnosing PTSD must be a snap. The person has lived through some traumatic experience, and now has certain symptoms: flashbacks, emotional numbness, and extreme jumpiness. What's so hard about that?

SMOKESCREENS

One trouble is, certain other psychiatric conditions often occur along with PTSD, and these can act as smokescreens. In other words, a doctor may notice and diagnose these other conditions (they're called coexisting conditions), but miss the diagnosis of PTSD. It's a pity when this happens, because it means the person probably won't get the ideal kind of therapy.

For instance, many people with PTSD drink too much. To the casual observer they seem like alcoholics, pure and simple. But when they enter alcoholism treatment programs, such people tend to do poorly. They may drop out. They may complete the program but then quickly go back to drinking. Or they may sober up, but continue to suffer from PTSD symptoms such as panic attacks, insomnia, violent fits of temper, paranoia, or emotional numbness.

People like this are not "pure" alcoholics; they need a treatment program that addresses more than just alcoholism. In fact, they need specific therapy for their PTSD. If they don't get it, they probably won't derive the maximum benefit from whatever therapy they do receive.

Since alcoholism and drug addiction are the two main smokescreens that obscure PTSD, let's take a look at each of them.

ALCOHOLISM

It's a fact that many people with PTSD drink too much. The obvious question is, are they suffering from PTSD or alcoholism?

DEFINITION

Alcoholism, by definition, is chronic compulsive drinking—often of more alcohol than the person intended. Besides doing considerable damage to physical health, alcoholism may interfere with a person's ability to make a living and to get along smoothly with family, friends, and coworkers.

Sixty-five percent of all Americans drink alcohol to some extent. Although many have less than three drinks a week, fully 13 percent of adults abuse or become dependent on alcohol at some point.

What's confusing is that alcoholism can take many different patterns. Some alcoholics drink every day. Others drink sporadically, or at predictable intervals (such as every weekend). However, there *is* a common denominator: In any kind of alcoholism, episodes of drinking clearly interfere with a person's normal functioning.

Symptoms

Alcoholism initially starts out as ordinary social drinking, but then progresses to a pattern of heavier and more frequent drinking. People who are sliding into alcoholism need more and more alcohol to get the desired effect; this is called the development of "tolerance."

Alcoholics deny that they have a drinking problem, even when the problem is obvious to others. Eventually they suffer from insomnia, anxiety, or depression, and blackouts (an inability to remember certain things that happened while they were drunk.)

Alcoholics have digestive problems and show signs of poor nutrition. Prolonged heavy drinking can cause tremor, high blood pressure, heart problems, and enlargement or even cirrhosis of the liver. Male alcoholics are prone to impotence.

Financial problems, frequent job changes, car accidents, and legal problems are common among alcoholics. Many alcoholics rely heavily on tranquilizers or other drugs. Some are suicidal or at times violent.

Sorting Out Alcoholism and PTSD

Alcoholism may cause some of the same symptoms as PTSD, but there are differences, too.

Many alcoholics suffer from insomnia, for example, but they generally do not have the intrusive ("hot") symptoms that characterize PTSD: flashbacks to a past traumatic experience, recurrent nightmares about the trauma, or extreme mental distress every year on the "anniversary" of the trauma.

Alcoholics may have memory lapses, and are likely to let drinking interfere with their relationships with family and friends. But in and of itself, alcoholism does not tend to produce the avoidant ("cool") symptoms characteristic of PTSD: a feeling of detachment from human beings, trouble experiencing any emotions at all, or a what's-the-use attitude stemming from a pervasive feeling that their life may end at any moment.

And although alcoholics may be irritable and subject to outbursts of anger, they don't typically show the increased-arousal symptoms that are hallmarks of PTSD: hypervigilance, an exaggerated startle response, or extreme panic when exposed to a specific reminder. (In PTSD, for instance, a woman who was raped in a stairwell may panic every time she enters a stairwell.)

Treatment

Treatment for alcoholism starts with medically supervised *detoxification*, which means going through physical withdrawal from alcohol. Then comes correction and prevention of nutritional deficiencies and cirrhosis.

After detoxification, it's time for long-term recovery work, which is called *rehabilitation*. Group psychotherapy can help break through alcoholics' denial that they have a drinking problem. Self-help groups such as Alcoholics Anonymous, which offer moral support and companionship, have helped millions of people recover from alcoholism.

Treatment for Both Alcoholism and PTSD

When a person who has a drinking problem is also suffering from the aftereffects of a trauma, it's impossible for a doctor to separate the effects of drinking from the delayed effects of trauma. It's also impossible for such a person to receive effective psychotherapy, for the simple reason that alcohol interferes with the ability to think and carry through on decisions.

From a practical standpoint, whether alcoholism developed before or after a traumatic event makes little difference: For the sake of mental *and* physical health, it's essential for the person to stop drinking.

You may recall that Ruth, the Navy nurse mentioned in Chapter Two, sought individual psychotherapy after treatment for alcoholism failed to calm her nerves, insomnia, and daytime flashbacks of her Vietnam trauma. Ruth *was* an alcoholic, and she definitely needed to stop drinking. But she also needed to work through her PTSD—and that required additional therapy of a different kind.

Ideally, a person whose PTSD is complicated by a drinking problem will first go through alcohol detoxification, and then receive therapy for both PTSD and alcoholism.

DRUG ADDICTION

Many people with PTSD are dependent on, or addicted to, mood-altering drugs other than alcohol. In many ways, what you've just read about alcoholism applies equally to drug addiction.

Definition

Drug addiction (or drug dependence) is defined as self-destructive behavior that stems from lack of control over the use of mood-altering drugs. Addicts keep taking drugs even though they are suffering from unpleasant physical, psychological, or social consequences.

As with alcoholism, drug dependence produces "tolerance," so that more and more is needed to get the desired effect. It's common for addicts to be dependent on two or more drugs at a time. For example, cocaine causes anxiety, so cocaine addicts may also use—and become addicted to—alcohol, tranquilizers, or heroin.

Symptoms

Stimulant drugs, such as cocaine, can cause effects identical to the "hot" symptoms of PTSD: anxiety, panic, suspiciousness, and aggressive or violent behavior. Marijuana and the sedating drugs such as heroin can cause effects identical to the "cool" symptoms of PTSD: withdrawal from people, apathy, lethargy, loss of drive and ambition.

Addicts have no control over how much of a drug they use, and no desire to control it. They spend most of their time acquiring drugs by whatever means necessary, often including theft. Family, friends, work, and usual activities go by the board as they concentrate on getting and staying high.

When addicts can't get drugs, they suffer from withdrawal symptoms. These vary from one drug to another. Some withdrawal symptoms are reminiscent of PTSD symptoms: anxiety, sweating, insomnia, irritability, restlessness, and depression. Others include nausea, vomiting, blurred vision, aching muscles, diarrhea, and seizures.

Sorting Out Drug Addiction and PTSD

Like alcoholism, drug addiction differs from PTSD in that it usually develops by itself, not as the result of a trauma.

Drug addicts in general do not suffer from those "hot" symptoms that characterize PTSD: flashbacks, nightmares about a particular trauma, or distress on the "anniversary" of a trauma.

Addicts who abuse sedating drugs such as marijuana or heroin may have memory problems because their minds are clouded by drugs. And addicts typically do put drugs before family and friends. But addiction itself does not tend to produce those "cool" symptoms characteristic of PTSD: a sense of being cut off from other people, an inability to experience emotions, or a feeling that their life will be very short.

People addicted to stimulant drugs, such as cocaine or amphetamines, may have insomnia and angry outbursts. While high, they may also show a PTSD-like increase in their level of nervous arousal: hypervigilance and an exaggerated tendency to startle. But their anxiety is diffuse, unlike the anxiety of PTSD which centers around a particular past trauma.

Treatment

Treatment for drug addiction, just like treatment for alcoholism, starts with *detoxification* to eliminate the drug or drugs from the body. Sometimes it's necessary to give antidepressant or anticonvulsant medication to ease this early period of recovery. Some detoxification programs also use medications that may diminish the addict's craving for a drug.

Then comes the longer-term part of therapy, *rehabilitation*. Initially, this should include individual counseling and group therapy. Later, membership in a self-help group such as Narcotics Anonymous can help addicts stay away from drugs and manage their impulsive behavior.

Treatment for Both Drug Addiction and PTSD

Again, as with alcoholism, drug addiction can mimic some of the symptoms of PTSD, making it impossible for a doctor to tell which symptoms (i.e., anxiety, flashbacks, withdrawal, lack of motivation) are caused by drugs and which are caused by PTSD. So when a patient has survived a traumatic experience and is also dependent on drugs, it's important to *treat the drug problem first*.

When the addict has gone through detoxification and is fully engaged in a rehabilitation program, if certain psychological and physical discomforts persist, the doctor can be more confident that those are indeed delayed effects of trauma—and can start treatment for PTSD in addition to the ongoing drug rehabilitation treatment.

MIMICRY

You've just seen how alcoholism and drug addiction, which so often coexist with PTSD, can act as smokescreens that cloud the diagnosis and treatment of PTSD. Now it's time to consider *mimicry*, which is a different sort of problem.

Mimicry occurs when the symptoms of PTSD "mimic" symptoms of another psychiatric disorder. This can lead a doctor to make the wrong diagnosis, especially if the person with the problem is confused or uncommunicative. There are four main psychiatric disorders that PTSD can mimic: major depression, manic-depression, generalized anxiety disorder, and panic disorder. Let's look at each in turn.

MAJOR DEPRESSION

You've already read that the "cool" symptoms of PTSD—such as withdrawal and lack of interest in ordinary activities—

can mimic symptoms of the psychiatric condition known as *major depression*. Here's a brief description of major depression.

Symptoms

People with major depression feel despondent (or perhaps irritable, in the case of children and teenagers) for most of the day, every day, for two weeks or more. They're either unusually restless or else noticeably slowed down in their ordinary movements, and they're no longer interested in people or daily activities. They may lose or gain considerable weight (more than 5 percent of their body weight within a month). They may either sleep all the time or complain of insomnia. They feel guilty or worthless; they may think seriously of suicide, or at least tell themselves that they want to die.

Of course, depressed feelings are natural after a loved one dies, and in that case the diagnosis of major depression doesn't apply. But if the mourner becomes caught up in feelings of worthlessness or thoughts of suicide, or "shuts down" and can no longer function even many weeks after the death, this may be bereavement complicated by major depression.

Delusions or hallucinations may sometimes occur during major depression. They may jibe with the depressed mood, centering on themes of guilt, pointlessness, or illness. Or they may be completely unrelated to the depressed mood, centering on themes such as control by outside forces, persecution, "insertion" of thoughts into the brain, or "broadcasting" of private thoughts so that other people can hear them.

How Major Depression Differs from PTSD

Major depression is primarily a *mood* disorder, without the intrusive symptoms (flashbacks, preoccupation with a past trauma) or heightened-arousal symptoms (extreme nervousness, tendency to start easily) of PTSD.

However, treatment that's appropriate for major depression may be a helpful part of therapy for people whose PTSD involves many avoidant symptoms, such as emotional detachment and withdrawal from others.

A few decades ago, psychotherapy was the only available treatment for major depression. Today, there are several different classes of antidepressant medications that can be very useful in helping to treat this disorder.

MANIC-DEPRESSION

Sometimes the "hot" symptoms of PTSD mimic the manic phase of a condition called *manic-depression*. Here's a short introduction to that disorder.

SYMPTOMS

Manic-depression, which is also called bipolar disorder, involves mania followed by depression.

"Mania" in this case means a high, cheerful mood (sometimes shifting into irritability) accompanied by wild ideas, loud and fast talking, easy distractibility, and little or no need for sleep.

Depression includes the symptoms described under the heading "major depression": low mood, decreased energy, feelings of worthlessness, loss of interest and pleasure in daily activities, appetite and sleep disturbances, and possibly thoughts of suicide.

The hallmark of manic-depression is the *shift* from mania to depression—but the shift can follow various patterns. For example, some people shift rapidly between a high and a low state; others may have one episode of mania followed by several bouts of depression, with normal periods in between.

How Manic-Depression Differs from PTSD

Mania may superficially resemble some of the "hot" symptoms of PTSD. But people experiencing a manic episode generally feel expansive, confident, and good about themselves, whereas people experiencing the intrusive symptoms of PTSD (flashbacks, nightmares, or distress on the "anniversary" of a trauma) find their symptoms disturbing and frightening.

Of course, a person who already suffers from manic-depression may live through a traumatic experience and then develop PTSD on top of the original disorder. This combination condition may be obvious enough to a doctor who has known the patient all along. But it can present a real puzzle to a doctor who meets the person only after the traumatic event has occurred, and who has no inkling of the underlying manic-depression.

One possible diagnostic clue: Lithium, a medication that can prevent manic episodes for 70 to 90 percent of people who suffer from manic-depression, is likely to be ineffective in people whose "manic episodes" are really caused by the intrusive symptoms of PTSD.

GENERALIZED ANXIETY DISORDER

Since anxiety is one of the symptoms of PTSD, here is a synopsis of a psychiatric condition called *generalized anxiety disorder*.

SYMPTOMS

People with generalized anxiety disorder are plagued by restlessness and needless worries, and suffer from chronic tension and anxiety. Their hands shake, they have dry mouth, they feel restless, and they have frequent, unexplained muscle aches. Their hands are sweaty or clammy. They're prone to episodes of racing heartbeat and "smothery," breathless feelings. They're likely to complain of chills or hot flashes, dizziness, upset stomach, and the need to urinate frequently. They are edgy and irritable, they startle easily, they have trouble concentrating, and they're plagued by sleep problems.

HOW GENERALIZED ANXIETY DISORDER DIFFERS FROM PTSD

Generalized anxiety disorder often does involve daydreams about unpleasant possibilities, but the daydreams don't focus on a *past* trauma, as they do in PTSD. To put it the other way around, flashbacks and nightmares centered on a past traumatic experience are common in PTSD, but do not play a part in generalized anxiety disorder.

Also, avoidant symptoms such as social withdrawal and lack of emotional depth, which form a part of the PTSD picture, are absent in generalized anxiety disorder.

PANIC DISORDER

People with PTSD often panic at the sight or sound of something that reminds them of a past trauma. Therefore, it's useful to compare PTSD with the psychiatric condition known as *panic disorder*.

Symptoms

People with panic disorder have recurrent, spontaneous attacks of extreme panic. Initially these attacks appear out of the blue, and not in response to any particular object or situation. Afterward, there is a period of intense fear of having another panic attack.

People who have a condition known as *panic disorder with agoraphobia* are so afraid of having an embarrassing panic attack that they routinely avoid all kinds of public places and situations.

Panic disorder is now widely recognized as a biochemical disorder involving a particular area of the brain. Medication, particularly tricyclic antidepressant medication, is the most effective therapy discovered so far.

How Panic Disorder Differs from PTSD

In panic disorder, the panic attacks are spontaneous, at least at first. These attacks are baffling precisely because they are not the result of any traumatic event. In contrast, PTSD-related panic attacks typically center on very specific memories of a traumatic experience. Thus, a person who nearly drowned may panic at the prospect of going for a swim; a person who survived a tornado may panic at the approach of a summer thunderstorm.

BURIED MEMORIES AND AMNESIA

Of course, when a highly disturbed person comes for therapy soon after surviving a traumatic experience, the diagnosis of PTSD is likely to be straightforward. But remember, PTSD doesn't always develop immediately after a trauma. Sometimes it takes months or even years for the symptoms to surface. When this happens, the condition is called *delayed-onset PTSD*.

People with delayed-onset PTSD were initially able to repress their feelings about, and even to some extent their memory of, the trauma they survived. But eventually, perhaps in response to some kind of stress, the feelings and memories came bubbling to the surface, causing repeated nightmares, attacks of rage, emotional numbness, or other troublesome symptoms.

Curiously, people with delayed-onset PTSD may have no idea what's causing their sleep problems and emotional difficulties. This is especially true if the trauma was *sexual abuse*. Why? Because victims of sexual abuse are sometimes so ashamed of what happened to them that they bury the memory very deeply in their minds. If a doctor asks them point-blank, "Were you ever sexually molested or abused?" they may even say, "No, never"—not because they're deliberately lying, but because their conscious mind has no access to the shame-filled memory. This lack of conscious memory of the trauma is called repression, or "selective amnesia."

• • •

You've seen how alcohol or drug abuse can complicate PTSD, and how PTSD can mimic the symptoms of, or even blend in with, other psychiatric disorders. By now you may be wondering about the natural history of PTSD—how it evolves in a person who receives no diagnosis and no treatment of any kind. This is an important subject that deserves its own chapter.

CHAPTER FIVE

THE NATURAL HISTORY OF PTSD

Let's talk about what happens to people with post-traumatic stress disorder who get no diagnosis, no counseling, no psychiatric help. Is PTSD a self-limiting condition? In other words, do people eventually get over PTSD all by themselves, given enough time?

The answer is: usually not. The following is a true story.*

BLOOD AND FLAMES

In 1986, 43-year-old Michael Dean and the woman he was living with, 32-year-old Caroline Hull, drugged Caroline's three young children with 30 ground-up sleeping pills. They blocked the driveway to keep fire trucks away, and doused their house with kerosene. Caroline then took an overdose of sleeping pills, and lay down with her children on a mattress in the basement. After Michael had shot the unconscious woman and her children, killing each of them with a

* O'Connor, Colleen, with Doherty, Shawn, "A Vietnam Vet's Suicide Pact," *Newsweek*, March 17, 1986, p. 30.

bullet to the heart, he set fire to the house. As the flames crackled, he finally turned the gun on himself.

Soon family members, the local newspaper, and even Congressmen received notes Michael had mailed just before committing the grisly murder-suicide. "We the veterans, widows and children of veterans are a forgotten group," the notes said.

According to the news report, some doctors thought Michael was "a textbook example" of PTSD. He had suffered a psychological breakdown while serving in Vietnam seventeen years earlier. He had married and divorced three times. He sought isolation, struggled with nightmarish memories of the war, couldn't hold a job, and spent most of his time writing bitter grievances to Congress about the way the government neglected Vietnam veterans.

Obviously, Michael's emotional condition did not clear up by itself. Instead, it consumed him and his loved ones in blood and flames. If, as suggested, he suffered from PTSD, the victims of the trauma included an entire family.

LONG-TERM DAMAGE

Fortunately, not everyone with PTSD ends up like Michael. Many, however, are crippled by serious, long-lasting psychological damage:

Marcia, who was mugged and raped five years ago, is so jumpy that the sound of an ambulance siren can make her drop her cup of coffee. She suffers from unexplained stomach pains, pelvic cramps, and joint aches; doctors can never pinpoint a specific physical disorder, and her own family thinks she's a hypochondriac. Marcia has irrational fears about her children, insisting that even her 17-year-old daughter be home every night before dark.

Ramiro, who escaped from imprisonment in his South American homeland after seven months of torture, began drinking to alleviate his emotional pain. Ten years later, alcoholism had completely taken over his life. He eventually joined Alcoholics Anonymous and has now been sober for three years. Yet he still has flashbacks to his prison experience, he's still subject to murderous fits of temper, and he still has to sleep with a light on at night.

Chris was married to a man who was prone to psychotic rages. One day her husband beat her savagely, locked her in a closet, and then shot and killed himself; Chris remained imprisoned in the closet until police officers broke into the apartment two days later. In the years that followed this personal catastrophe, Chris married and divorced three times. She has serious memory lapses, finds it impossible to concentrate, and has never held a job for more than a few weeks. Her two children, who were suffering from severe neglect and mistreatment, were placed in a foster home. Chris feels isolated, lonely, and guilty.

NATURAL HISTORY OF RECOVERY

Many people who are temporarily devastated by a major trauma do make a complete recovery. How do they do it? One well-known theory maintains that the "natural history" of *recovery* from a trauma follows a stepwise course.

First comes the *catastrophe* itself—whether it's a natural disaster, an accident such as a plane crash, a combat experience, or a mugging or other crime. The catastrophe phase, intense and horrifying, is over once the victims feel they are out of immediate danger.

Then come *relief and confusion*, as the victims realize they escaped death but wonder why and how. At this point, if others died in the catastrophe, the victims may start to feel guilty and unworthy.

Then there is a period of *avoidance* that helps the victims get over their anxiety. A person who survived a horrible automobile crash may avoid driving or even getting into a car. Someone who lived through an accidental explosion in a factory may take a prolonged disability leave. A woman who was raped may avoid going outside alone.

Next comes *reconsideration*, in which the victims confront their trauma—fearfully, at first—rather than avoiding everything that reminds them of it. The person who survived the auto accident decides to start driving again. The survivor of the industrial accident goes back to work at the plant. The rape victim ventures outside by herself once again.

Finally comes *adjustment*, in which those who have lived through a catastrophe make the transition from "victims" to "survivors." They are able to carry on their lives as they wish, unhampered by psychological roadblocks related to the trauma they experienced.

PTSD: A "SHORT CIRCUIT"

Catastrophe . . . relief and confusion . . . avoidance . . . reconsideration . . . and adjustment: That's the sketch of *normal* recovery from a trauma. In PTSD, though, it's as though something *short-circuits* the normal recovery process. Those automatic reactions to sudden catastrophe—racing heart, quick breathing, adrenaline coursing through the blood—remain on hair-trigger alert. Relief about surviving gives way to raw nerves or depressed rumination. Avoidance patterns become a way of life.

What determines whether a person who lives through a trauma will recover fully, partially, or not at all? The jury is still out on this question. Some doctors believe the answer lies in the nature of the disaster: The worse the trauma, the greater the likelihood that the survivors will develop PTSD. Other doctors think the answer lies in the nature of the person: Certain types of people seem more likely than others to make a good recovery from disaster.

DOES EDUCATION MAKE A DIFFERENCE?

Oddly enough, there is statistical evidence that people's *education level* affects how well they cope with the aftermath of disaster. Scientists studying former prisoners of war discovered that better-educated men from middle-class backgrounds generally showed more resilience after captivity than men who had never graduated from high school.*

Why should education make any difference? No one knows for sure. It may be that better-educated people are more able to think objectively, put their situation in perspective, and make the most of any opportunities for recovery.

Lady Borton, the author of *Sensing the Enemy*, spent years helping direct a Quaker relief operation in Asian refugee camps where children were dying of malnutrition. Today, more than a decade later, she is still susceptible to intrusive memories of her experiences in the camps. She says it's as if two movie projectors are always running in her head simultaneously. Usually she focuses on the "movie" of the present, but occasionally a certain sight or sound will switch her attention to the "movie" of the past.** One day, for

* Bower, B., "Emotional Trauma Haunts Korean POWs," *Science News*, vol. 139 (February 2, 1991), p. 68.

** Borton, Lady, "Ambushed by Memory, We Seek Refuge, in Vain," *New York Times*, January, 28, 1988, p. C2.

example, as she was pushing her cart through the produce aisle in a supermarket,

> The second movie projector in my mind shifted on screen. Suddenly I was back pushing a cart of protein supplements through a refugee camp . . .

In her mind's eye, Lady Borton then saw an image from her own past: a badly malnourished child lying naked in the dirt of the camp.

> With her bloated belly, she looked like a butternut squash cast out on a compost pile. I pushed on with my cart of supplements, knowing that within hours the child would be dead. In the supermarket, I see that child as I push my cart past tiers of choices. Her face takes over cans of baby formula and boxes of cereals.

Lady Borton's personal account suggests that PTSD is not an either-or proposition (i.e., something that a person either has or doesn't have), but occurs *along a continuum*. A highly educated woman, Lady Borton—who does not consider herself to be suffering from PTSD—has had to learn to control the flow of haunting memories that stem from her work in the refugee camps. Mirrors, for some reason, tend to open the floodgates on those memories:

> It's easy enough in my own home to avoid known stimuli, like mirrors. In a restaurant or a friend's house, I have learned to choose a place briskly before I'm the last one seated. I settle down with the mirrors behind me, the way a combat veteran may sit with a wall at his back, his face toward the unpredictable entrance.

Perhaps it's not so much education level, but psychological sophistication, that allows people like Lady Borton to identify "trigger" stimuli, control them, and thus soften the impact of traumatic memories and flashbacks. Some people seem to develop this sophistication on their own. Others can learn it with the help of specific therapy for PTSD.

WELL-ADJUSTED OR NOT?

Predictably, perhaps, the people who tend to recover from a catastrophe quickly and completely are those who were well-adjusted before the trauma occurred.

In 1983, disastrous bushfires in Australia damaged or destroyed some 385 ranches. Flames, whipped by winds strong enough to snap large trees, mounted to heights of 200 yards. Twenty-eight people died, many hundreds were injured, and some 250,000 animals were lost in the flames.

Later, researchers studied 469 volunteer firefighters who had fought the blaze. They found that for the first few months after the fire, most of the firefighters were highly distressed by disturbing memories and flashbacks. However, only 20 percent of the firefighters went on to develop PTSD. Many of these men, it turned out, had suffered from either depression or unusual anxiety at some time *before* the bushfires occurred.

In other words, the firefighters who were well adjusted before the disastrous blaze got over their trauma and got on with their lives. But those who were psychologically disturbed or fragile before the fire erupted were less able to shake the horror of the trauma. They got bogged down in flashbacks, nervousness, jumpiness, imagined aches and pains, depression, and alcoholism.

SPOTTING THE VULNERABLE VICTIMS

According to research in the United States, people who live through a major trauma are at above-average risk for developing chronic, disabling PTSD if they:

1. Are *"neurotic,"* i.e., tend to become anxious or depressed easily; or
2. Have *obsessions*, or come from a background in which other family members suffer from obsessions; or
3. Have a history of *behavior problems* in childhood and early adolescence (e.g., frequent fighting, truancy, vandalism, delinquency, running away, early sexual experience, and alcohol or drug abuse).*

People with problems like these tend not to bounce back to normal after a disaster. Their built-in emotional fragility cuts down on their ability to roll with the punches. Months after fellow trauma survivors are back at work and leading normal lives, these people are still struggling with disturbing memories, disabling nervousness, and energy-sapping insomnia. They have PTSD, or are on their way to developing it.

BLINKS AND DREAMS

Research shows that in the wake of a severe trauma, increased levels of arousal can persist for many months, even in those survivors who do *not* develop PTSD. Often the increased arousal is barely noticeable, or perhaps even totally invisible, to the casual observer.

---

* Helzer, John E., et al., "Post-traumatic Stress Disorder in the General Population," *New England Journal of Medicine*, v.317:26 (December 24, 1987), pp. 1630–34.

For instance, brain researchers studied a group of Los Angeles children who had been present when a demented sniper opened fire on their school playground, killing two youngsters and injuring several others.+ A controlled experiment showed that when these children were exposed to sudden bursts of "white noise," they blinked more rapidly than children who had not actually witnessed the violence. None of these children had PTSD. Yet some of them had the speeded-up blinking response for as long as twenty-one months after the attack.

Eventually, though, the children did return to normal. What was it that finally calmed down their nervous eyeblink response to bursts of noise? In a more general sense, what is the physical or mental maneuver that allows many trauma survivors to overcome their increased nervous arousal, and thus avoid the development of PTSD?

One possible answer is complete *repression* of distressing memories, and even of dreams. An Israeli study of Nazi Holocaust survivors showed that those who were well adjusted, suffering from no mental or physical illnesses, were remarkably unaware of their own dreams.* Monitoring in a sleep laboratory pinpointed the times when these Holocaust survivors were having rapid-eye-movement (REM) sleep, the stage of sleep when vivid dreams occur. Yet when researchers awakened these people from REM sleep and asked them to recount their dreams, they couldn't do it—and insisted that they hadn't been dreaming at all!

Besides repressing their ability to recall dreams, these researchers reported, well-adjusted Holocaust survivors tend to keep their emotions in check and put their concentration-

+ "Tracking Children of Violence," Washington Post, Sept. 5, 1989, p. WH20.

* Bower, B., "The Repressed Road to Trauma Recovery," *Science News*, vol. 136 (July 1, 1989), p. 4.

camp memories in cold storage. Keeping a tight emotional grip on themselves seems to protect them from the potential ravages of PTSD.

Is "keeping a tight grip" something people can learn in therapy? That's a controversial issue. As you'll learn in an upcoming chapter, most therapy for PTSD concentrates not on repression and tight control, but on recall and relaxation.

DELAYED ONSET

In some people who live through a catastrophe, PTSD symptoms lie mysteriously dormant for months or even years, finally erupting after a stressful event such as divorce, a job loss, or the death of a loved one. People with this *delayed-onset* type of PTSD probably had some "hot" (hyperarousal) or "cold" (avoidance) symptoms dating back to the original trauma, but were able to *repress or cope* with them for an extended period of time. But when they encountered extra stress, they finally "cracked"—and developed the symptoms of full-blown PTSD.

It's amazing how thoroughly some people, especially young children, are able to repress the memory of a trauma. A dramatic real-life example came to public attention in 1990, when 29-year-old Eileen Franklin-Lipsker told California police officers that twenty-one years earlier she had watched her father sexually assault and bludgeon to death an 8-year-old girl who was her friend.*

Eileen said her father warned her that no one would believe her if she told what he had done to her friend, and that he would kill her if she did tell. Eileen not only told no one, but successfully repressed the memory of her father's crime. The murder remained unsolved for two decades.

* "Daughter's Repressed Memory," *Wall Street Journal*, October 12, 1990, p. B8.

Then Eileen, who had meanwhile developed symptoms of PTSD, underwent therapy. It was during a therapy session that she suddenly remembered the grisly scene her mind had worked so hard to forget.

Psychiatrists believe that many cases of delayed-onset PTSD go unrecognized, especially those that involve children's repressed memories of a trauma.

CHILDREN'S TRAUMAS, SEXUAL OR NOT

Children are particularly likely to repress memories of *sexual* trauma. It's important to remember that boys as well as girls can be victims of sexual abuse. Boys who were sodomized often grow up to be sexual abusers themselves, even if they no longer have any conscious memory of the abuse they experienced. Some girls who were molested or raped become prostitutes when they're older, whether or not they remember their early sexual trauma. Others have children who, in turn, fall victim to sexual abuse.*

Repressed memories of *any* childhood trauma, sexual or not, may eventually "pop out" as part of delayed-onset PTSD. This became particularly clear in January 1991, when televised images of the Gulf War terrified immigrant children whose families had fled from wars in their homelands.

Teachers in Los Angeles reported that some immigrant children who had been "A" students found the newscasts of the Gulf War so unbearable that they were suddenly failing tests.** Counselors saw normally well-behaved immigrant children who suddenly refused to obey, lost their ability to pay attention, and burst into uncontrollable tears at odd

* Meer, Jeff, "Violence and Mental Illness," *Psychology Today*, Feb. 1985, p. 11.

** Hamilton, Denise, "Reliving Terror," *Los Angeles Times*, Jan. 28, 1991, p. B1.

moments of the day. Psychologists warned teachers and counselors that immigrant children, depending on their background, might react to the televised Gulf War reporting with anything from mild apprehension all the way to PTSD with full-blown panic attacks.

OTHER PEOPLE'S REACTIONS

There's yet another element involved in the natural history of PTSD, and that's the way other people treat survivors of a trauma.

With the wisdom of hindsight, therapists think one reason why so many young Americans who served in Vietnam developed delayed-reaction PTSD was the cold-shoulder reception they got when they came home to the U.S. Large numbers of people who opposed the continued U.S. involvement in Vietnam snubbed and insulted veterans who returned. Many ex-soldiers thus came home from battle only to find that "home" had become a hostile environment. For some, the ongoing stress of this unfortunate situation proved unbearable, and the result was delayed-onset PTSD.

However, outright hostility isn't the only reaction that can demoralize survivors of a disaster. After a car wreck, a mugging, or a rape, for example, well-meaning family members and friends often deal with the victim by trying to *minimize* or make light of the emotional impact of the trauma—under the assumption that talking about it will only make things worse.

Although this "minimizing" tactic springs from kind intentions, it often does more harm than good. Survivors whose friends and relatives "minimize" soon get the idea that they should deny their own feelings and thoughts about their harrowing experience. Instead of working through the trauma, they "stuff" their emotions and try to bury their harrowing memories. All too often they end up depressed and anxious—and if they use alcohol or drugs to medicate their discomfort, this only compounds the misery. Eventually, when such people get around to seeking therapy, they may not even realize that their basic problem is delayed-reaction PTSD.

Speaking of therapy, you're probably wondering what therapy can do for people suffering from PTSD. That will be the next topic.

CHAPTER SIX

BEARING THE UNBEARABLE

One truly encouraging fact about post-traumatic stress disorder is that it's an eminently *treatable* condition. As you'll see in later chapters, the right kind of therapy can work wonders—even for people who have lived through seemingly unbearable tragedies, suffer from severe PTSD, and describe themselves as "nervous wrecks."

WHY GO FOR THERAPY?

Why go for therapy? The psychological reasons are compelling. Before therapy, people with PTSD live in a mental world of discomfort and seemingly imminent danger. Therapy teaches them, basically, to *bear the unbearable*. In therapy, they learn to confront discomfort, work through it, and then turn their energy toward new goals and satisfactions.

Gabriel is a South American political refugee who in his home country was beaten, drugged, and subjected to hours of interrogation under spotlights. For ten years after coming to the U.S., he had a visceral reaction to any bright lights. "One time I went for a dental appointment," he said, "and when the dentist turned on his examining light I jumped out of the chair and ran from the building. I couldn't help myself." Gabriel's home life was stormy; he periodically flew into rages and beat his wife. His three young children were afraid of him. His violent temper sometimes flared up at work, too: He lost four jobs in a row because of fistfights with coworkers. Torture had left him with a profound sense of helplessness, which sometimes expressed itself as episodes of deep depression.

Now, after six months of intensive therapy for PTSD, Gabriel is functioning better at home and at work. When he feels himself getting angry, he warns his wife that he's "having a PTSD attack" and that she should leave him alone. When she wants to talk with him about a problem, and he feels like pulling away, the two of them make an appointment to talk later. Gabriel has started a local chapter of Amnesty International; lobbying foreign governments to free political prisoners helps him get beyond his crippling feelings of helplessness.

No one, including Gabriel, claims that six months of treatment have "erased" his memories of torture. But therapy has helped him feel better about himself, revise his attitude toward life, and function more comfortably and effectively both at home and in the larger world. To Gabriel, those psychological benefits make the effort of therapy seem well worth while.

STRESS AND PHYSICAL ILLNESS

Another compelling reason why people with PTSD should seek therapy is that unrelieved stress is bad for their *physical* health.

You'll recall that in PTSD the nervous system remains on "stress alert," at the brink of the fight-or-flight reaction, long after the actual trauma has passed. An abnormally prolonged state of alert appears to be hard on the whole body. Evidence for this comes from a 1986 study of police officers in Buffalo, New York.*

The Buffalo study, which recognized that law enforcement agents routinely encounter and deal with violence throughout their careers, compared police officers with municipal employees whose jobs were less stressful. Results showed that, as the years went by, the policemen had exaggeratedly increased rates of *heart disease*—particularly the kind caused by hardening of the arteries. They also had significantly higher-than-expected rates of *cancer*. Their rates of *circulatory and digestive problems* were much higher than rates for other municipal workers. When compared to people in other occupations, police officers had the third highest rate of *suicide*. And their overall rates for *injury, illness, and fatality* were higher than for any other occupation.

What apparently wore down these police officers' immune systems, and damaged their overall health, were chronic rushes of adrenaline, caused by repeated on-the-job exposure to violence.

Although most people with PTSD aren't police officers, they do have something in common with them: chronic rushes of adrenaline. If, as seems likely, these repeated fight-or-flight reactions do damage the body's resistance to physical disease, that's an excellent reason to seek treatment for PTSD.

FOR THE SAKE OF THE FAMILY

PTSD inevitably causes behavioral problems that wreak havoc on family life—problems such as sexual difficulties, fits of

* Anderson, Wayne, and Bauer, Barbara, "Law Enforcement Officers: The Consequences of Exposure to Violence," *Journal of Counseling and Development*, vol. 65 no. 7 (March 1987), p. 381.

rage, emotional coldness, groundless anxieties, and alcohol and drug abuse. For their own sake, the family members should do everything they can to ensure that the person with PTSD enters therapy.

One very common problem in PTSD is the inability to become sexually aroused. A woman whose PTSD is the result of rape by a stranger, for example, may find she has lost all interest in having sex with a man—even her husband. In self-defense against her feeling of helpless vulnerability, she walls off her sexual responsiveness. Her husband, misinterpreting her reaction, thinks she's trying to tell him that he's inadequate as a lover. Within their marriage, this sets up a vicious circle of rejection, hurt, and anger. Therapy for PTSD can help straighten out this kind of destructive pattern within a relationship.

A man with PTSD may sometimes look to sex as a tranquilizer to soothe his raw nerves. If he tries to move directly to intercourse, skipping the "time-wasting" preliminaries, he's likely to shock and offend his partner. She may give in resentfully, just to keep the peace. Or she may pull back in anger, at which point he may get angry and even abusive. Once again, these are the types of destructive patterns that PTSD therapy can help correct.

But sex is only one of many PTSD-related family problems. And spouses aren't the only ones who suffer; children do, too.

A peculiar thing happens to some children of people with PTSD: They experience what's called *secondary traumatization*. Even though they did not live through the trauma that scarred their parent, they seem to absorb many of the parent's jumpy reactions and irrational fears.

Thus, when Wanda developed PTSD after she was attacked and raped in an elevator, 12-year-old Sherrie started copying many of her mother's morbid fears. Sherrie, like Wanda, refused to use an elevator. She became afraid to walk outside unescorted. Even when she was out in the company of other people, she was preoccupied by the need to make it home well before nightfall.

In this case, Wanda wasn't the only one who needed therapy. Sherrie also needed help, to overcome the irrational fears linked to her secondary traumatization.

Both spouses and children may suffer the fallout from the emotional numbing that's so characteristic of PTSD. To limit the degree of stress on their already hyperstimulated nervous system, most PTSD sufferers go through periods when they seem incapable of communicating normally. They don't talk—not even enough to make sure daily routines will go on.

Jeff, for instance, began to suffer form serious PTSD symptoms several months after he survived an industrial accident that killed his best friend. Although Jeff had always given his children a ride to school in the mornings on his way to work, he suddenly began "forgetting" them. Without any warning, he would simply get into his car after breakfast and drive off to work without them. In one part of his mind, Jeff knew very well that he was disrupting a routine and making his children late for school. But that part of his mind seemed remote, inaccessible. He was no longer tuned in to his children and their needs; his concerns centered on himself. When his wife and children indignantly confronted him about these peculiar morning lapses, he shrugged. To him, it didn't seem worth talking about.

In PTSD, these unemotional, non-communicative episodes are linked to depression and feelings of hopelessness. Therapy for PTSD can help people like Jeff recognize, cope with, and eventually overcome such emotional "whiteouts."

HOPE FOR THE FUTURE

Do families usually realize what a difference PTSD therapy can make? Yes, they're usually convinced as soon as they begin to see the results in their loved one. Gradually, as the weeks pass, bafflement, annoyance, and anger give way to understanding, tolerance, and cheerfulness—in other words, hope for the future.

One woman said of her husband, a combat veteran, "Before my husband began PTSD therapy, neither of us knew what was wrong with him. He blamed society for all his problems and I blamed him for all of mine.

"... When we were having our rough times, my parents and friends kept urging me to leave him. But I had faith in him and felt that counseling could help. And it has.

"... PTSD counseling hasn't gotten rid of my husband's symptoms. But it has made them much more manageable.

"[He] still gets depressed, and angry, but not as often and not for so long. His nightmares are almost gone.... We even talk now."*

EARLIER IS BETTER

Since PTSD is rooted in the biology of the physical reaction to stress, the problems it causes become more and more deeply ingrained as time goes on. That's why it's important for people who have lived through a trauma to get counseling as soon as possible—preferably before delayed reactions such as panic attacks, insomnia, heavy drinking, and emotional withdrawal turn into harmful patterns.

It's important for families to realize the importance of

* Matsakis, Aphrodite, *Vietnam Wives*. Rockville, MD: Woodbine House, 1988.

therapy, because many people who survive a catastrophe are very reluctant to seek help, or even to accept it when it's offered. Survivors tend to want to show that they can cope. They may think accepting therapy of any kind will prove them "weak" or, worse yet, "mentally ill." It helps a great deal if family members point out that counseling is available, that it's likely to be helpful—and that a little therapy right away may prevent a great deal of psychological discomfort in the future.

Chapter Seven

Mapping Out a Safety Zone

You may remember Guy, described in Chapter Two, who developed post-traumatic stress disorder after he was attacked and stabbed while sleeping in his car by the ocean. Guy spent three weeks in a hospital recovering from his stab wounds. But after his release, it was only a week before he found himself back in the hospital—this time a psychiatric hospital. You may be wondering why Guy needed to be *hospitalized* for PTSD treatment. Should everyone with this disorder spend time in a hospital?

The answer is: No, hospitalization isn't always necessary. Partly, the decision of whether to hospitalize depends on how severe the PTSD symptoms are. But partly, too, the decision depends on how *safe* the person feels.

NOWHERE TO RUN, NOWHERE TO HIDE

Guy was essentially homeless. He had lost his apartment some months earlier, which was why he had been living temporarily with married friends. But the friends were an unhappy couple, and their arguments—which sometimes degenerated into physical abuse—disturbed him so much that he was desperate to escape. On the night he was attacked, he had been camping out in his car simply to avoid sleeping at their house.

After leaving the first hospital, Guy's first order of business should have been to find a place to stay. But going back to the home of his married friends was too depressing to contemplate. Moving in with his brother occurred to him as a possibility, but since he and his brother had never been very close, he had neither the inspiration nor the emotional energy to make the request. Guy spent that first night on a park bench, unable to sleep and unable to think what he should do next.

He spent the rest of that week in the park, too, in a kind of daze. At the end of the week, one of the nurses who had cared for him in the hospital happened to walk through the park and was shocked to find him there—unwashed, unshaven, hungry and disoriented. She alerted the hospital social worker. By the end of that day Guy had been admitted to Oak Creek Hospital, which is how I first met him.

The reason Guy needed to be hospitalized was that he had become, in medical jargon, "dysfunctional": He had temporarily lost the ability to take care of his basic physical needs for food, clothing, and shelter.

The trauma of the brutal attack had occurred while his life was in a state of flux: On that particular night, sleeping in his car, he had been not only jobless but essentially homeless, and also disturbed by the tense, violent atmosphere at his friends' house. Three weeks later, when the hospital released him, he still had no job and no place he could call home.

Worse yet, the attack had stirred up very old, very disturbing memories from his childhood. As he lay in a hospital bed recovering from the beating and stabbing, Guy wasn't consciously *thinking* of the day when he and his brother cowered helplessly as their father murdered their mother and her lover. But the *feelings* from that long-ago trauma were coming back, washing over him like ocean waves on a sandy beach. He felt very small, very helpless, and very alone in the world. He felt that no one really cared about what happened to him. He felt that what he said or did made little difference—that his life would always be ruled by unfriendly forces that were beyond his control. He felt unsafe.

Thus, even though Guy's stab wounds had healed enough to permit him to leave the hospital, his psychological state had deteriorated seriously. He was isolated, defenseless, and too deeply mired in practical difficulties to see a way out.

Guy was a clear example of someone whose PTSD mimics major depression. It's true that he was depressed. But more than that, he was overwhelmed by confused, helpless feelings dating back to the family trauma he had lived through as a child. His PTSD had taken an *avoidant* turn. Although he did have insomnia, and recurring nightmares of being beaten and knifed, his main PTSD symptom was a gradual emotional shutdown—a growing inability to communicate his basic needs. Guy felt as though he were seeing the world from inside a glass mask. Increasingly, it seemed to him that he would never be able to get back on his feet, find a job and a place to live, and function as a normal person again. In his mind, he had nowhere to run, nowhere to hide.

A SAFE HOUSE

Psychiatric hospitalization can be a godsend for someone like Guy. Since the hospital assures such basics as food and shelter, and keeps each patient on a tightly planned daily schedule, it prevents the kind of languishing that Guy fell into during his week in the park. The hospital's intensive schedule of psychotherapy helps bring buried psychological problems out into the open; talking about the problems makes them seem less overwhelming, more manageable. Patients relate to one another in group meetings and therapy sessions, which helps break through the type of crippling social isolation that was affecting Guy. Also, the hospital provides a nonthreatening, trusting atmosphere where people like Guy can acknowledge and "process" their recurrent nightmares and intrusive thoughts.

In short, the psychiatric hospital functions as *a safe house* for people who no longer feel safe on their own. Until these people rediscover their ability to manage their own lives, the hospital takes over for them, allowing them to relax about issues of physical survival so that they can concentrate on fulfilling their pressing psychological needs.

REGAINING TRUST

To continue with the story of Guy, one of the main tasks in therapy was helping him regain a sense of faith in himself and trust in other people.

Hospitalization was a basic step; while he was living at the hospital, at least he didn't have to struggle for survival. The next step was helping him find an emotional "safe place" in his individual therapy sessions with me.

Since Guy had come from an unsafe, unnurturing environment, he didn't automatically look to me as a potential friend and helper. In our first conversations he was polite, but distant and reserved. He certainly didn't trust me enough to admit to any feelings of anger or fear about what had happened to him that night by the ocean.

I started individual therapy with Guy by asking him to tell me the story of his life, and to describe what events had led to his admission to Oak Creek. This process, which is called "taking a history," is an essential preliminary to any extended course of psychotherapy.

Guy cooperated, going back to his childhood and recounting the story of his mother's sudden violent death, his father's arrest and disappearance, and he and his brother's journey away from home and into foster care. He continued by recounting his rather uneventful growing-up years, his marginally adequate career as a carpenter and handyman, and his confusion and perplexity when the bottom fell out of the job market, leaving him without work or a place to live. He told of moving in temporarily with his married friends, and discovering the ugly reality behind their "happy couple" facade. And he ended with the story of the brutal attack by a band of thugs who robbed him and left him for dead.

As he told me these facts, Guy maintained a casual, almost complacent tone of voice. He had lived through a tremendous family catastrophe in childhood, and a recent, shattering criminal attack. Yet he wanted to give me the impression that these events were really not a big deal to him—that they were nothing out of the ordinary, and that he could easily take them in stride.

To maintain his sense of control, Guy adopted the intellectual position that the negative events in his life were all more or less normal and *understandable*. His married friend had threatened him with a revolver? "Well, yeah," said Guy, "but you have to understand, this is a fellow who gets drunk a lot. He doesn't always know what he's doing."

As part of his effort to remain in control, Guy even assumed a burden of guilt. He had been robbed, beaten, and abandoned by the seaside? "Well, yeah, but in a way it was my fault," he told me. "I had no business sleeping out there on the cliffs. It was stupid. I could have gone and slept at my brother's, I guess, and it would have saved me a lot of hassle."

It took at least two weeks of daily individual psychotherapy sessions before Guy would admit to any fear, helplessness, or anger about the misfortunes in his life. Gradually, he and I got past his defenses, and he began to feel safe enough to express negative feelings. He acknowledged some anger toward the married couple in whose house he had temporarily lived: "They were basically jerks," he told me. And he admitted that he felt angry toward his brother: "He knew I had lost my apartment, and he could have invited me to move in with him for a month or two. But he didn't. And even though I pretended it didn't matter, that did hurt."

At this point, I knew that Guy was on his way to getting better. He was beginning to trust me, which meant he was finding emotional safety within the therapeutic relationship.

SOCIALIZING WITH PATIENTS

So in the hospital Guy had found a safe physical environment, and a therapeutic relationship where he felt safe enough to acknowledge emotions such as anger and guilt. Next he needed to expand his "safe place" to include social relationships—starting right there in the hospital.

A patient in an ordinary hospital may or may not converse and become friendly with staffers and other patients. What's unique about psychiatric hospitalization is that social life—in other words, relating to the nurses, therapists, and other patients on a daily basis—is a built-in part of the therapy. The guiding philosophy is that people with psychiatric disorders can't get better in a social vacuum. They need other people as friends and sounding boards.

Psychiatric hospital community meetings, which convene every morning, and group psychotherapy sessions, which are part of every patient's daily schedule, keep patients in touch with other people and give them automatic feedback on how they're doing. Loud, disruptive individuals soon receive the subtle or not-so-subtle message that their boisterousness gets on people's nerves. Timid, retiring people soon find themselves in confrontation with others who want to know what they really think and where they really stand.

For Guy, the group sessions in the hospital were a big change from the solitary life he was used to. Speaking up in a group intimidated him, but as he got used to it, he gained self-confidence. Better yet, the more group sessions he attended, the more amazed and relieved he was to discover that there were other people with problems like his.

In group therapy he met Bob, a trucker who had survived a vehicle crash in which another driver died. Like Guy, Bob tended to avoid people and was out of touch with his emotions. And like Guy, Bob tended to blame himself for the misfortunes that had befallen him.

At first Guy could clearly see Bob's "avoidant" behavior, but not his own. After a few weeks in the group, however, Guy started catching himself in some of those avoidant behavior patterns. Gradually, as he developed the ability to face people rather than hide from them, he found himself opening up emotionally. It felt good. Guy could tell that his therapy was leading him to change in helpful ways.

TAPPING INTO A COMMUNITY NETWORK

The goal of hospital therapy was to get Guy ready for "life on the outside." At one time he had been a fairly committed Christian, but over the years he had gradually slid away from involvement with his church. Once Guy was comfortable with his social relations within the hospital community, he was ready to renew his links with people outside the hospital. One day, in individual psychotherapy, he told me that church activity used to be important to him, and that he wouldn't mind renewing that involvement.

A few days later he was able to attend a Sunday service at his old church, and came back visibly cheered. Over the next several weeks he renewed his acquaintance with a number of church members. He was asked to join an evening Bible study group, accepted after some hesitation, and came to enjoy the weekly sessions.

Soon after Guy's discharge from the hospital, the church steering committee, aware of his carpentry skills, agreed to pay him to renovate the kitchen in the parish hall. He did a good job, and word got around. Other churches in town began offering him similar work, and by the end of that year Guy had as much business as he could handle. He had pulled himself out of his financial slump, was renting a decent apartment, and—best of all—had a reasonably full social schedule for the first time in his life.

FINDING ACCEPTANCE

A sense of acceptance is a crucial human need. Whereas people with strong family ties usually feel a sense of belonging, individuals like Guy, who lack those family ties, have to find acceptance elsewhere. Guy's troubled childhood had made him so emotionally cautious that he tended to be a loner. As long as his life proceeded smoothly, this worked out all right. But when he ran into financial hard times, he had little sense of how to reach out to people for help. Then, when he fell victim to a violent crime, the trauma and disorientation only increased his social isolation. A very important part of Guy's PTSD therapy was determining which people he liked and trusted, and learning ways to let these people into his life.

In light of what psychiatrists now know about the importance of acceptance, it's no wonder that large numbers of Vietnam veterans developed PTSD. Not all of these young men participated in the horrific My Lai massacre or its equivalent; many of them had war experiences that were considerably less traumatic than that. But thanks to the burgeoning antiwar movement, many Vietnam vets encountered wholesale social rejection when they got back to the U.S. That sustained lack of acceptance made them feel unwanted and abandoned—and the resulting isolation set the stage for PTSD.

After any severe trauma, whether war-related or not, the quality of the reception "back home" can go a long way toward calming—or worsening—survivors' emotional damage. Trauma victims who return to an environment that soothes them, supports them, and bolsters their self-confidence are the lucky ones. Those who return to an environment of indifference or even hostility are less fortunate. These are the people most likely to develop full-blown PTSD, and most likely to need at least some time recovering in a psychiatric hospital.

To return to our original question, you can see that hospitalization isn't a must for *every* person suffering from PTSD. But for those whose PTSD symptoms are severely incapacitating, and who lack a safe, secure home environment in which to recover, a psychiatric hospital can be a welcome and very beneficial temporary haven. Effective recovery from PTSD starts with a feeling of personal safety. In some cases, the hospital is the place that can best provide that sense of security.

Chapter Eight

Hand Over the Happy Pills

So what's the scoop on medication—is there a pill that can cure post-traumatic stress disorder?

Not really. Despite all the recent advances in medications for the mind, there's still no magic bullet that can knock out PTSD the way penicillin knocks out a strep throat—and there probably won't be such a pill in the foreseeable future. The reason: In bacterial or viral infections, microbes attack one particular part of the body. But in PTSD, severe trauma upsets the balance of the mind and the body, affecting many organ systems all at once.

That said, though, there *is* a place for medication in the treatment program of some people with PTSD—particular medications for *anxiety, depression,* or *psychosis*. None of these medications can cure the whole syndrome of PTSD. But a well-chosen medication may alleviate certain troubling PTSD symptoms, and thus clear the path for psychotherapy to do its work.

For any given patient with PTSD, when is it right to give medication, and what medication will work best? These questions lead to an area where, from a doctor's point of view, the practice of medicine becomes as much an art as a science.

EARLY ON: DANGER OF MASKING

Let's begin by considering when medication is *a bad* idea. In the hours following a severe trauma, it's psychologically very normal for the survivors to be emotionally upset. Some victims may be intensely fearful; others may feel rage. Some victims may act depressed; others may withdraw and show no emotion at all. Some victims may feel like killing whoever they think was responsible for the catastrophe; others may feel like killing themselves. Many simply go over the catastrophe in their heads, "seeing" it happen again and again. Some victims may sit stock still as if paralyzed by shock, while others pace the floor and wring their hands in agitation.

At this point, compassionate people who want to help may assume that a dose of a sedative will do the victims good. But the truth is that victims of physical traumas, such as a plane crash or earthquake, should *never* receive psychiatric medication before undergoing a very thorough physical evaluation. That's because people emerging from such a trauma may have *hidden brain or nerve damage*.

Naturally, people with massive brain damage have problems that are very obvious to everyone: They may be comatose, or paralyzed on one side of the body, or unable to remember their name, age, or address. But people suffering from more subtle brain damage may have only slight, seemingly trivial symptoms—perhaps headache, drowsiness, blurred vision, or a stiff neck.

Thus, in the wake of physical trauma, it's crucial to withhold all psychiatric medication until tests have ruled out injuries such as a fracture of the skull, a subdural hematoma, or tissue or vascular damage to the brain. Injuries of these types can sometimes cause symptoms that look just like psychological or "nervous" responses to severe trauma. But psychiatric medications won't make such symptoms go away.

Worse yet, the medications could *mask the symptoms* of any brain or nerve damage that might have occurred. The problem is that psychiatric medications frequently cause lethargy or confusion. If a trauma victim starts taking medication before undergoing a thorough physical exam, and then shows symptoms such as sleepiness in the middle of the day or difficulty holding a conversation, the doctor won't know how to interpret these symptoms. Are they signs of brain damage—or simply side effects from the medication? It will be difficult or impossible for the doctor to know for sure.

Marita, for instance, was rescued from a burning building, but her three-month-old baby perished in the flames. Concerned relatives immediately gave Marita tranquilizers, hoping to help her cope with her grief. What they didn't know was that a falling beam had glanced off Marita's head, causing a pool of blood to collect beneath her skull and press against her brain. When she complained of dizziness, the family put her to bed, assuming she was reacting to the pills. Several hours later, they realized that she was comatose. They rushed her to the hospital, where an emergency operation relieved the pressure on her brain—but not in time to prevent a minor degree of brain damage. If no one had given Marita tranquilizers, her brain injury would have been obvious much earlier, and she might have escaped brain damage altogether.

LATER: TO MEDICATE OR NOT

Assuming that a very thorough physical exam has ruled out the possibility of brain damage, how does a doctor decide which victims of severe trauma need medication and which victims should do without?

Once the immediate trauma is past, the doctor's rule of

thumb is to consider giving medication to people whose post-trauma reactions prevent them from coping with ordinary, everyday life. Here are some examples:

SEVERE AGITATION. Sarah, a frail woman in her eighties, was the victim of a brutal mugging. In the hospital, days after the attack, she was still so agitated that she couldn't sit still. Despite the cast on her arm, she paced constantly, wandered the corridors when she could, and at one point almost fell down a flight of stairs. Sarah was a candidate for a short course of a sedating medication.

SEVERE ANXIETY. Donna was raped one night on a dark street, and several days later had the first panic attack of her life. Soon she was having a panic attack at least once a day. For 15 or 20 minutes at a time she would suffer from a racing heart, tingling hands and feet, pain in her chest, and a terrifying feeling that she was about to die. She would continue to feel tense and anxious for hours after each attack. Donna was a candidate for a short course of antianxiety medication.

PERSISTENT INSOMNIA. Glenn, an employee at an amusement park, had the job of taking tickets and operating the on-off controls of a fast-moving ride. One day a freak accident occurred: A cable broke and a teenage boy plummeted to his death. Although Glenn had not caused the equipment to malfunction, he was overcome with feelings of guilt. Memories of the horrible accident kept him awake at night, and nightmares marred the little sleep he did get; during the day, he was so tired he felt like a zombie. Glenn was a candidate for a short course of sleeping medication.

SUICIDAL DEPRESSION. Will and Nancy were abroad, vacationing at a newly built hotel, when disaster struck. Owing to a construction error, part of the hotel collapsed, sending an avalanche of glass and concrete into the elegant lobby. Will, who happened to be walking through the lobby just then, was one of five people killed by the cave-in.

Nancy was inconsolable. As the weeks and months passed, she lost weight and continued to feel helpless and hopeless. Six months after the accident her depression turned suicidal; she became preoccupied with plans to take her own life. Nancy was a candidate for a long course (six months or more) of antidepressant medication.

DELUSIONAL THINKING. Harry, who was kidnapped in a Middle Eastern country, lived through a prolonged trauma of torture, imprisonment, and ill treatment before he was finally released. Back home, he suffered from severe PTSD with paranoia: He believed that the walls of his house were bugged, and that foreign spies could hear every word he uttered. Harry was a candidate for a short course of an antipsychotic medication.

MEDICATION POSSIBILITIES

Doctors who prescribe medication for patients with PTSD have four basic categories to choose from:

- Medications that act on the peripheral nervous system
- Medications that act on the central nervous system
- Medications that regulate emotions, such as lithium and carbamazepine
- Antidepressant medications, including tricyclic antidepressants and monoamine oxidase inhibitor (MAO) antidepressants

Let's take a look at each category, and see how these capsules and tablets work.

PERIPHERAL NERVE MEDICATIONS

Two medications that may be useful in PTSD, clonidine and propranolol, work on the peripheral nervous system.

Clonidine (brand name, Catapres) is given to some people who have high blood pressure, but it has psychiatric uses, too. Technically clonidine is classified as an alpha blocker. This means it acts on alpha receptors, which are tiny sensitive spots within certain brain cells.

Buried deep within the brain is an area called the locus ceruleus which is chock-full of alpha receptors. When the locus ceruleus cells are excited, they beam out distress signals that cause an exaggerated startle response, panic, sweating, flashbacks, and *hyperarousal* in general. Normally, these locus ceruleus cells are kept quiet by the body's own supply of a natural chemical called norepinephrine. When a trauma occurs, the body pumps out an extraordinary amount of norepinephrine to keep the locus ceruleus cells under control.

The trouble starts once the trauma is over. Because the body's supply of norepinephrine is temporarily all used up, the cells in the locus ceruleus go berserk, beaming out distress signals which cause the hyperarousal symptoms of PTSD. Clonidine calms down these cells by blocking the alpha receptors—that is, fitting onto the alpha receptors to satisfy them.

The results are swift and impressive. Right away the panicky feelings, sweating, and excessive tension melt away. Clonidine is not an instant cure for PTSD—but it allows the person to be calm, receptive, and capable of benefitting from psychotherapy.

Propranolol (brand name, Inderal) is best known as a medication that's given to prevent second heart attacks; however, like clonidine, it also has psychiatric uses. Technically propranolol is classified as a beta blocker. This means it acts on beta receptors—tiny sensitive nerve spots which, when excited, command the adrenal glands to release adrenaline.

Adrenaline is the hormone that's responsible for the well-known fight-or-flight response. When disaster strikes, it's the rush of adrenaline that momentarily lets ordinary people accomplish superhuman feats of strength: run as fast as a professional racer, lift impossibly heavy objects, jump unusually high.

Once again, the trouble is likely to begin after the trauma has passed. With the body's supply of adrenaline momentarily depleted, the beta receptors cry out for more adrenaline. Their clamor causes shaking knees, tense muscles primed for action, and perhaps nightmares or a rush of uncontrollable anger—those all-too-familiar hyperarousal symptoms of PTSD.

Propranolol nips this process in the bud by fitting itself onto the beta receptors, satisfying them so that they stop crying out for more adrenaline. As with clonidine, the results are remarkably swift. The person relaxes, stops shaking, and no longer feels impelled to rush into reckless action. Like clonidine, propranolol treatment is not a cure for PTSD—but for trauma victims who are plagued by inappropriate fight-or-flight reactions, it's a helpful step toward getting ready for psychotherapy.

Neither clonidine nor propranolol is a perfect medication for people with PTSD. Although these drugs can help calm anxiety, reduce the exaggerated startle response, and prevent nightmares, they may also cause low blood pressure, drowsiness, and fatigue in some people. In addition, propranolol sometimes interferes with sexual arousal, causing impotence or lack of desire.

Ideally, a person with PTSD who takes a peripheral-nerve medication such as clonidine or propranolol will need it for only a few weeks or months. Once the cycle of hyperarousal has been broken, the person can go off the drug and rely on psychotherapy to complete the treatment for PTSD.

CENTRAL NERVOUS SYSTEM MEDICATIONS

Other medications that are sometimes helpful in treating PTSD are the *benzodiazepines*. These drugs work not on the peripheral nerves, but on the central nervous system. They include diazepam, alprazolam, lorazepam, and oxazepam. Let's examine each of these.

Diazepam (brand name, Valium) and *Xanax* (alprazolam), probably the most-prescribed tranquilizers in the United States, work by inhibiting the action of the central nervous system—that is, the brain and spinal cord. Diazepam is remarkably fast-acting, reaching its peak activity a mere 20 minutes after the pill is swallowed. Alprazolam is less likely than diazepam to cause drowsiness. Both of these compounds induce calm, promote sleep, and reduce nightmares. What could be bad? They sound like perfect medications.

Unfortunately, that's not the whole story. For one thing, benzodiazepines and alcohol don't mix; taken together, they depress the central nervous system so much that they can actually cause a person to stop breathing.

For another thing, the benzodiazepines are addictive drugs. And people with PTSD—many of whom are already "medicating" themselves with alcohol, marijuana, or other drugs—are especially apt to get addicted to these tranquilizers.

A related problem is so-called cross-tolerance between alcohol and the benzodiazepines. People who have been using either alcohol or a tranquilizer for some time eventually start to need bigger doses to get the effect they're used to; this is called the development of tolerance. It turns out that people who already have a high tolerance to alcohol—as many hard-drinking PTSD victims do—automatically have a high tolerance to benzodiazepines. The term for this is cross-tolerance. People who are trying to kick alcoholism are warned to stay away from tranquilizers to avoid developing a double addiction.

For these reasons, doctors are extremely cautious about giving benzodiazepines to people who have PTSD. If they prescribe them at all, they usually specify a short course. They may insist that PTSD patients sign a contract stating that they will take this medication for only two weeks, at the very start of their therapy.

Oxazepam (brand name, Serax) and *lorazepam* (brand name, Ativan) are other varieties of benzodiazepines. They take effect more slowly than diazepam, and wash out of the body more quickly. Like diazepam and alprazolam, however, they also have a calming effect, promote sleep, and can reduce or eliminate nightmares.

EMOTION-REGULARING MEDICATIONS

Lithium and carbamazepine, medications that work on the body's emotion-regulating mechanism, sometimes prove helpful to some people with PTSD.

Lithium, a naturally-occurring mineral, is best known as a treatment for manic-depression. Contrary to popular belief, lithium isn't a mood elevator at all. Its main function is to prevent the development of the wild, excited, out-of-control state known as mania.

For people with manic-depression, the manic state may seem interesting and exciting—but eventually there's a rebound effect, with mania giving way to grim, painful depression. When lithium is taken faithfully over the long term, it keeps the emotions on an even keel. By preventing the peaks of mania, it also prevents the valleys of depression.

As you read in Chapter Four, manic-depression develops of its own accord, not in response to any particular trauma; as a psychiatric condition it's considered to be quite distinct from PTSD. Interestingly, though, PTSD and manic-depression sometimes respond to the same kind of medication. Some people with PTSD who feel emotionally out of control, always on the verge of exploding, regain a sense of self-control when they take lithium.

In one clinical trial, 14 out of 22 Vietnam veterans with PTSD benefited from lithium therapy. On lithium, they lost their tendency to react to ordinary stress as if it were a repeat episode of their original trauma. They were also able to cut down on their excessive drinking.

Carbamazepine (brand name, Tegretol) is best known as an anti-epilepsy medication, but is also used to treat manic-depression. Like lithium, carbamazepine can soothe the hyperarousal symptoms of at least some people who suffer from PTSD. And like the tricyclic antidepressants that are its chemical relatives, carbamazepine can counteract the withdrawn, emotionless, "cool" state that overtakes some PTSD victims.

Both carbamazepine and lithium may cause dizziness, stomach upset, or double vision. But whereas lithium sometimes causes tremor, extreme thirst, and frequent urination, carbamazepine doesn't usually produce these unwanted effects. Thus, carbamazepine may be an alternative for certain PTSD sufferers who can't tolerate some of the side effects of lithium.

Since lithium is non-habit-forming, it can be taken for long periods of time with no danger of abuse or addiction.

Unlike the benzodiazepines, both lithium and carbamazepine are meant for long-term therapy. Patients who take them need periodic blood tests, however, to make sure the dosage they're taking is still the dosage they need.

ANTIDEPRESSANTS

By now you know that hyperarousal is only one half of the PTSD equation—the "hot" half. The "cool" half is a dull, withdrawn, depressed state that some doctors call *constriction*.

People whose PTSD takes the predominantly "cool," constricted turn tend to be silent, uncommunicative, zombie-like, and possibly suicidal beneath their emotionless facade. For them, the best choice of medication may be an anti-depressant.

Antidepressants are sometimes called mood lifters. Contrary to what you might suppose, though, they are not stimulant medications. They work by correcting imbalances in the body's own natural "mood chemicals." If you are depressed, the right antidepressant can rearrange the proportions of mood chemicals in your body so that you feel normal again. But if you're already in a normal emotional state, an antidepressant won't make you feel "on top of the world." In fact, it probably won't do a thing for you.

People with PTSD who are handicapped by depression feel hopeless, can't concentrate, and have no interest in or enthusiasm for anything. Most doctors think it's important for such people to take an antidepressant, to enable them to pay attention to and benefit from psychotherapy.

Sometimes a blood test can help the doctor decide which antidepressant is likely to be most helpful. But in many cases, the most valuable clue in choosing an antidepressant is simply the experienced doctor's clinical expertise. Here are some of the most common choices of antidepressants:

Imipramine (brand name, Tofranil), which is one of a class of medications known as the *tricyclic antidepressants,* not only regulates the body's mood chemicals but also has a sedating effect. This medication is most likely to help depressed PTSD patients who can't get to sleep at night, have no appetite, and are losing weight. Improved sleep is usually one of the first benefits of therapy.

Imipramine may take as long as three weeks to reach maximum effectiveness, so it's important not to give up on it too soon. In the early weeks of therapy, frequent blood tests are necessary to help the doctor determine the right dosage. Depending on the results of the blood tests, it may be necessary to increase or decrease the number of pills per day.

One disadvantage of imipramine is that an overdose can be quite dangerous. Since depressed people sometimes use overdoses of pills in suicide attempts, doctors are usually careful to prescribe only a small amount of imipramine at a time.

Another disadvantage of imipramine is that it occasionally causes heart problems. No one with a known heart condition should take this medication without a doctor's careful evaluation.

Imipramine can cause uncomfortable side effects such as dry mouth, constipation, urinary retention, sweating, and blurred vision. Starting with a low dosage, and gradually increasing it, can help minimize these side effects. Also, some side effects tend to disappear as the body gets used to the medication.

Other tricyclic-type antidepressants that doctors may prescribe for people with PTSD include *doxepin* (brand name, Sinequan), *nortriptyline* (brand name, Pamelor), and *amytriptyline* (brand name, Elavil).

Fluoxetine (brand name, Prozac) is one of the newest antidepressants on the market. So far, it seems to be about as effective as the tricyclic antidepressants, but has the advantage of causing fewer side effects. Some people, however, do experience side effects from Prozac. The most common ones are nausea, headache, insomnia, and agitation.

Phenelzine (brand name, Nardil), an entirely different type of medication, belongs to a class of antidepressants known as the *monoamine oxidase inhibitors*, or MAOIs. It combats depression by causing the body to accumulate certain natural mood-regulating chemicals called amine neurotransmitters.

Phenelzine is most likely to help depressed PTSD patients who have panic attacks or phobias, who eat to soothe their nerves, and who are gaining weight. Ideally, the medication will help such people feel calmer and regain their ability to experience pleasure.

Unfortunately, however, a few PTSD patients who try phenelzine actually feel more aggressive than ever, and are bothered by unusually frequent flashbacks or intrusive recollections of their trauma.

One major disadvantage of phenelzine is the dietary restrictions that go with it. People who take phenelzine must avoid all foods and drinks that contain a substance called tyramine. A few examples of things to avoid would be aged cheese, cured meats and fish, yogurt, red wine, and beer. Consuming any of these may lead to a fierce headache and dangerously high blood pressure.

Another disadvantage of phenelzine is that if the medication fails to work, it isn't possible to just switch overnight to a tricyclic-type antidepressant such as amitriptyline, a fourteen-day "washout" period is necessary to protect the body from harmful chemical interactions. As you can imagine, fourteen days can seem like forever to someone who needs relief from depression. So doctors are apt to try a tricyclic antidepressant first, and switch to phenelzine only if the first type of medication doesn't work.

Other MAOI antidepressants that doctors may prescribe for people with PTSD include *isocarboxazid* (Marplan) and *tranylcypromine* (Parnate). Like phenelzine, these medications require patients to stick to a tyramine-free diet.

GAINING PERSPECTIVE

To repeat: No medication can cure PTSD, but certain medications may relieve the severe psychiatric symptoms that cripple some victims of trauma.

One of the main functions of medication is to give trauma victims a psychological breather, allowing them to put emotional distance between themselves and the trauma. Once they are able to back off and gain some perspective on their experiences, they will begin to see the traumatic event not as part of a nightmarish present, but as part of *history*. At that point they will be able to take an active role in their own therapy, starting with some form of behavior modification—the next subject.

Chapter Nine

Back to the Scene of the Trauma

A youngster who's learning to ride a bicycle wobbles, falls, and wails. Her caring parent swiftly tends to the scraped knee, then helps her up on the bike again. Almost instantly the child forgets her tumble, and continues learning to ride.

That's a mild, everyday example of what's technically known as "exposure therapy." Horseback riders express the principle this way: If you fall off your horse, you should get right back on again before fear has a chance to set in.

At first it might sound trivial to mention bicycle and horse mishaps in a book about post-traumatic stress disorder. But in fact, the "get-right-back-on-again" principle can indeed apply in the treatment of PTSD. When people who have suffered through a traumatic experience emerge with a specific *phobia* or *avoidance pattern,* exposure therapy is an effective way to help them overcome that crippling pattern.

POST-ACCIDENT DRIVING PHOBIA

Jacqueline, for instance, was cruising down the highway on her way to a graduate school class when suddenly her world turned upside down. She hadn't seen the tractor-trailer creeping up behind her. When she pulled into the left lane to pass someone, her tiny subcompact car glanced off the advancing truck in a crack of metal-on-metal and a shower of shattered glass.

When she came to in a hospital emergency room, she had no clear notion of how the accident had happened—and at first she wasn't even sure of her own name and address. Her heartsick family feared she was brain-damaged. With attentive medical care, however, Jacqueline came around rapidly. Several days later she was home from the hospital, bruised and shaken but mentally intact. Her insurance paid for a new car, and within ten days she was ready to drive again.

Everything seemed fine until she got behind the wheel. Then, as she put the key in the ignition, the memory of the accident came rushing back to her. Terrified, she tore open the door of the car and ran into the house, sobbing, "I can't, I can't! I never want to drive again!"

Jacqueline's family was sympathetic. That week, her brother offered to take time off from work to drive her to and from her classes, and she gratefully accepted.

But the week stretched into a month, and then two and three months, as Jacqueline continued to shun driving. She tried out her new car once or twice, but soon gave it up: She was so nervous that she jerked the wheel wildly whenever she saw another vehicle approaching.

Half a year after the accident, Jacqueline still wasn't driving. She suffered from frequent headaches for which doctors could find no cause. During the daylight hours she was edgy and moody, and at night she was troubled by insomnia and nightmares of the accident. She had dropped out of school and was spending her time at home, sleeping until late morning and watching TV all afternoon.

Jacqueline was suffering from a specific trauma-induced

driving phobia. When she finally sought treatment for PTSD, an important part of her therapy consisted of overcoming the phobia and learning to drive again.

KEEPING A LID ON STRESS

The therapy wasn't nearly as simple as climbing back up onto a bicycle or a horse. Before there was any mention of driving, a therapist trained Jacqueline in *progressive muscle relaxation*. Once a week for three weeks, Jacqueline learned how to isolate different groups of muscles in her body and consciously relax them. She liked relaxation training because it felt good. Even more importantly, relaxation training gave her some control over nervous reactions that she used to think were automatic—reactions such as a racing heart, rapid breathing, and a feeling of doom.

In the second stage, which involved *visualization*, it was time to at least start thinking about driving. The therapist asked Jacqueline to imagine herself approaching her car . . . then getting into the car, turning the key in the ignition, engaging the gears, starting down the driveway, and so on. She asked Jacqueline to describe all of these imagined actions in as much detail as possible. At whatever point the fantasy began to seem frightening, Jacqueline was to stick with that image and simultaneously start her progressive muscle relaxation.

Bit by bit, Jacqueline was able to imagine herself driving down a quiet street, then navigating in-town traffic, and finally cruising along a highway, without dissolving into hysterical tears. She was mastering the "imaging" techniques that would help her overcome her driving phobia.

In the third stage, armed with her new powers of relaxation and visualization, Jacqueline took *action*—she actually started driving again. At first she only sat behind the wheel for a few minutes, imagining what it would be like to turn the car on. On the second day, with her brother beside her in the passenger seat, she started the engine, ran it briefly, then turned it off. On the third day, with her mother in the car, she headed down the driveway and back up. And on the fourth day, accompanied by her father, she drove around the block. She continued in this progressive fashion, using visualization to "see" herself driving without fear, and falling back on her relaxation techniques whenever panic threatened to overwhelm her.

By the end of the third week Jacqueline was fully comfortable with highway driving, and no longer felt she needed a member of the family in the car with her when she drove. Exposure therapy, combined with relaxation exercises, had helped her overcome her post-traumatic phobia of driving. An added benefit was her improved physical health: Once she was driving again, her chronic headaches disappeared and she began to sleep well. It wasn't long before she was re-enrolled in graduate school, and her life was back on track.

AVOIDANCE, DIRECT AND INDIRECT

Although Jacqueline's fear of driving was a very straightforward consequence of her car accident, avoidance patterns in people with PTSD are not always quite so clear cut.

Sam, for instance, who served in the Gulf War in 1991, survived the Scud missile attack that devastated U.S. Army barracks in the Saudi Arabian desert; his brain was seared with the memory of companions lying in pools of blood, either dead or screaming in pain. Back home again after the war, Sam developed a fear of supermarkets, movie theaters, and shopping malls. In response to his military trauma, he had slipped into an *indirect* avoidance pattern. He was no longer in danger of a Scud attack, of course. But unconsciously he felt that in any place where large numbers of people were gathered under one roof, a surprise attack might occur at any moment.

Fortunately, exposure therapy works regardless of whether the avoidance pattern is direct or oblique. When he entered therapy, Sam, like Jacqueline, first learned progressive deep relaxation. Then he was taught to visualize himself going into a supermarket—first for just a minute, then for a quick purchase, then for several items, and finally for a whole shopping cart full of groceries. When he was able to visualize these scenarios without overwhelming anxiety, he started the action phase—making actual forays into stores and theaters. At first he went with a companion and for short periods of time; later he ventured in by himself, in gradually lengthening excursions.

After a month of these exercises, Sam had overcome his phobia of enclosed public places; he was able to go anywhere he pleased and stay as long as he liked. Thanks to exposure therapy, he was once again a free individual, no longer psychologically stuck in a traumatic moment of the past.

WORKING WITH BEHAVIOR

In overcoming their specific post-traumatic fears, Jacqueline and Sam both benefited from what doctors call *behavioral therapy*—a branch of therapy that the public still knows little about. The theory behind behavioral therapy is simple: Get a person to act repeatedly in a constructive new way, and soon the new behavior will become a habit.

People with post-traumatic phobias or avoidance patterns have accidentally fallen into the habit of responding fearfully to a certain sight, sound, or situation. Behavioral therapy sets out very deliberately to break that habit, using a three-step approach.

- First, teach the person how to *relax* deeply and completely.
- Second, teach the person to *imagine* the feared situation, using deep relaxation to calm the anxious thoughts and feelings that arise.
- Third, teach the person to *seek and master* the feared situation, starting slowly and preparing the way with relaxation and visualization exercises. Once the situation becomes familiar, it will no longer call up the fear response.

Behavioral therapy is beautifully simple, makes intuitive sense, and has no harmful side effects. Best of all, studies have shown that it is quite effective. People who succeed in mastering behavioral techniques feel a surge of confidence as they leave their fears and phobias behind. They sense that they've gained a psychological skill, and they're right: If the fear ever recurs, or if they ever find themselves troubled by a new fear, they can rely on the same behavioral therapy techniques to pull themselves together again.

ONLY PART OF THE PROGRAM

Lest you think behavioral therapy is a panacea, let me add that it's usually *part* of a PTSD therapy program, not the whole program.

For one thing, PTSD patients may need medication first. Many people with post-traumatic phobias and avoidance patterns are too emotionally unstable to embark right away on the mental exercises that behavioral therapy requires. Such people are prime candidates for medication to help them calm down, collect their scattered thoughts, or focus their energy. Once they have gained this emotional stability, they'll be ready to learn the behavioral techniques that help banish irrational fears.

For another thing, they're almost sure to need "talk therapy," too. Most, if not all, people with PTSD are wrestling with complicated, unresolved questions about the cause and meaning of the trauma they experienced. Behavioral therapy is an excellent tool for overcoming avoidance patterns. However, it's too mechanical to help resolve profound, deeply personal issues. When it's time to look at the big questions, there's no substitute for the insights that come from careful, probing *psychotherapy*.

With that, let's turn now to psychotherapy, and examine the role it can play in the treatment of PTSD.

CHAPTER TEN

TELL ME A STORY

People with post-traumatic stress disorder need to talk out their feelings—it's as simple as that. Even if medication is very successful at lifting their depression or calming their nerves, even if behavior therapy allows them to leave anxieties or phobias behind, they still need to do a lot of talking with a skilled listener.

The reason: Mental trauma distorts people's sense of who and what they are. In a train wreck, a rape, or an earthquake, more than just flesh and bones are crushed; spirits are crushed, too.

You might think that victims of psychological trauma would emerge from their experience feeling triumphant, or perhaps shaken but grateful to be alive. But that's not how it usually works. On the contrary, very often these victims emerge feeling small and insignificant, overwhelmed by what happened to them. What's more, they're apt to feel somehow stained or tainted by the trauma, as if the experience were something shameful, something to hide.

Why is this so? It's because people need to believe that they're in control of their lives. When a traumatic event shakes that belief, they tend to fix the blame on themselves.

If they had done things differently, they reason, the disaster never would have happened—or at least, not to *them.*

For those who weren't involved in the trauma, it's easy enough to see the flaw in this reasoning. After all, accidents, natural disasters, and random crimes happen every day—often to good, kind people who "deserve" only the best in life.

But whether they admit it or not, most people who are beset by trauma find the notion of randomness highly threatening. They need to feel that the things that happen to them throughout life make sense. They prefer to believe that life metes out rewards to good people and punishment to bad people. Even though that train of thought is highly simplistic, it's very common. It's common because it's reassuring: It provides answers.

Thus, when survivors of psychological trauma feel guilty, ashamed, and diminished afterwards, at least part of the reason is that they are telling themselves: "Something bad happened to me. I must have deserved it."

A QUESTION OF CONFIDENCE

Another reason why many trauma victims are so deeply shaken is that they've lost the confidence they need to function normally. To understand this, let's look for a moment at the way life ordinarily works.

When you wake up in the morning, get out of bed, and stand up, the floor remains firm beneath your feet. When you twist the knob, the door opens. When you turn on the faucet, water flows into the sink. When you brush your teeth, your mouth feels fresh and tingly. All through the day, in thousands of tiny ways, things happen the way you expect them to. Even though you're not aware of it, all these insignificant little "things that go right" give you a certain confidence. It's nothing extraordinary, of course. It's just regular, necessary, garden-variety confidence—a feeling that you know your familiar everyday world and how to manipulate it to get what you need.

Now, just imagine how an overwhelming psychic trauma can dissolve that comfortable, ordinary confidence. In the U.S., rape and armed robbery are two of the most frequent traumas that precipitate a PTSD response. A woman named Bonnie had walked from her office building to her car hundreds of times with no problems. But everything changed one evening when, shortly after leaving the building, she was jumped from behind, knocked to the ground, kicked, raped, and robbed. Even weeks after the incident, that formerly safe, familiar route still felt like enemy territory to Bonnie. Her traumatic experience had taught her that she could no longer count on getting from her office to her car in one piece.

What's more, that one violent "learning experience" had called the rest of her life into question. Was she really a competent worker? she asked herself. Was she strong enough to handle the job she held? Was she even a normal, acceptable person? Maybe her true self was timid, weak, and ineffectual. Maybe there was something about her that invited violent attack. Surely she must lack something that other people had. Why else would those attackers have picked on *her,* and not someone else? Or perhaps she was cursed with bad luck. Maybe she was destined to be picked on again and again, all her life!

These negative, self-destructive thoughts went around and around in Bonnie's head. She felt contaminated, guilty, unworthy. The fabric of her personal integrity was in tatters. She needed to realize objectively how the violent attack had damaged her sense of herself. And she needed to reconstruct her ordinary, everyday confidence in herself and her capabilities.

This wasn't a job Bonnie could undertake on her own. She was completely demoralized, and besides, she had no idea where to start. She needed the skilled help of a trained therapist.

"NO ONE COULD POSSIBLY UNDERSTAND"

In psychotherapy for PTSD, one of the first hurdles to overcome is the trauma victim's belief: "No one could possibly understand what I've been through." That strong feeling of isolation, and possibly of contamination, acts like an invisible shield. It walls off the victim, making him or her hopeless about the possibility of getting back to ordinary happiness and contentment with everyday life.

Why is the victim so certain that no one could possibly understand? Well, the story of the traumatic event is often full of genuine horror. As the best-known psychiatry reference book so blandly puts it, trauma is by definition "outside the bounds of ordinary human experience." True accounts of binding and gagging and death threats, or crushed skulls, or deep gaping wounds, or vicious rape, are so disturbing that most untrained people can't listen to them for long. Casual listeners, and even well-meaning relatives and friends, may try to put an end to a trauma victim's grisly tale with soothing comments such as, "Well, dear, that's all behind you, so don't fret any more. You're safe and sound now."

The trouble is, swift reassurances encourage *repression* of disturbing memories. The victim of trauma soon finds himself thinking, "I guess they're right. There's no use talking about all this any more. It doesn't do any good. It upsets them to hear about it. And it makes me stand out as a freak."

So the victim clams up and doesn't talk about it any more. Inside, though, he's still a roiling cauldron of unresolved emotions: terror, anger, helplessness, grief. As you saw in earlier chapters, those raging emotions do manage to express themselves—as flashbacks and intrusive memories, or depression and avoidance, or a mixture of these symptoms. That's what underlies the emotional quagmire of PTSD. Experience has shown that the surest way for PTSD victims to get out of that quagmire is to *talk* their way out.

RELIVING THE TRAUMA

This is where "talk therapy" comes in. Psychotherapists aren't the only good listeners in the world, of course. But they do have special training in helping people recapture and relive, rather than repress, disturbing memories. Psychotherapy for PTSD involves just that: helping the victim relive the trauma in minute detail, literally minute by minute or even second by second.

The reason for reviving the traumatic memories, and examining them in great detail, is to *demystify* them. As you saw with Bonnie, the memory of the mugging and rape that she endured took on a sinister, "mystical" power. That memory diminished and devalued her in her own eyes, making her feel like a weak, incompetent, undeserving creature.

This wasn't logical—and in a way, that's just the point. Bonnie needed someone to take a mental walk with her back to the night of the crime. She needed help thinking it through bit by bit and talking it out. She needed help discovering for herself that what had happened to her on that night was simply one of life's freak occurrences, the result of being "in the wrong place at the wrong time." She needed help realizing that she had been, and still was, an intelligent, worthy, competent human being. She needed help talking her way back to a clear picture of herself as a valuable, deserving person who was free of blame for what had happened to her.

Here at the hospital, we begin psychotherapy for the PTSD patient by taking as deep a history as we can. We ask her to try to recall absolutely everything about the traumatic event—not just where and when it happened, but everything that led up to it, and every detail of how it unfolded.

Once she has told the full story as a narrative, we take the exercise further. We ask her to tell the story again, this time adding all the details about *what was going on in her mind* at the time of the events she describes. With Bonnie, for instance, we would ask her what she remembered about the people who assaulted her—what impression she had of them, the feelings she had about them, anything she noticed about them that evoked a response from her. This part of the storytelling can take many hours; trying to rush through it is a mistake. It takes time, plenty of time, to think back, recover the emotional details, and round out the picture of what happened.

FINDING A CONTEXT

Next comes the job of taking the traumatic event and putting it into the context of the PTSD victim's life. In Bonnie's case, the rape and mugging had come at a particularly bad time. Only a month before the incident, her mother had died. And not long before that, her long-term relationship with a man she cared for had started to disintegrate.

In therapy, as she talked about her life, Bonnie realized that the criminal attack had so devastated her partly because she had already been feeling depressed and tearful. The attack would have been traumatic under any circumstances, of course. But feeling alone and abandoned had made it impossible for her to bounce back the way she might have done in happier times. Instead, she spiraled downward into guilt and depression, had attacks of "nerves," and avoided people she knew.

To her surprise, Bonnie discovered that beneath her feelings of unworthiness lay a large measure of anger. She was angry at the thugs who had brutalized her. She was angry at the man who had left her for another woman. Startling as it first seemed, she found she was even angry at her mother for dying and leaving her alone.

Depression and repressed anger are common feelings in people who, like Bonnie, find themselves in difficulty without a sturdy support system to bolster them. The great value of psychotherapy is bringing these feelings out into the open, examining them, tracing them back to their origins, and demystifying or "defusing" them. This paves the way for the constructive work of rebuilding a personal support network—which you'll hear more about shortly.

Also, people often treat a person differently after she has lived through a traumatic experience. One familiar scenario goes like this: A woman is brutally raped by a stranger. Afterwards, her husband (or boyfriend) loses interest in sharing physical intimacy with her; he treats her as though she were "tainted goods." This attitude rubs off on her, and she begins to feel that indeed she is dirty and defiled by what happened to her, even though she was entirely blameless. Healing a damaged self-image is yet another problem to work on during psychotherapy.

IT REALLY *WAS* THE TRAUMA

A word to the wise: Both the patient and the therapist can expect to have some trouble dealing with the intense emotions of PTSD.

Most people with PTSD are initially very wary of sharing

the story of their trauma with a therapist. As you've seen, they tend to be convinced that no one can really understand what they've been through. Before sharing their story, they may test and retest the therapist to see if he or she is truly "trustworthy."

In addition, since trauma is by nature dramatic and unsettling, some psychotherapists get extremely uncomfortable when they hear at length about a patient's personal trauma. For the therapist, it may be tempting to blame the patient's symptoms on something other than the trauma. An uneasy therapist may look eagerly for evidence that the person was psychologically unbalanced *before* the traumatic experience. The therapist may then prescribe an antidepressant medication and hope that the medication alone will clear things up.

But no matter what psychological problems the person may have had before the traumatic event, PTSD is a real disorder that deserves recognition in its own right. Until proved otherwise, psychological problems that follow a severe trauma should be considered results of the trauma. And in any case, medication without "talk therapy" isn't enough to help a person overcome PTSD.

What's needed, then, is the trauma victim's willingness to trust and share, and the therapist's willingness to listen and believe. These are the mandatory conditions for successful psychotherapy for PTSD.

A LEARNING PROCESS

Once the person with PTSD has shared her full story, how can the therapist help her make sense of the traumatic event she has lived through?

For one thing, the therapist can teach her what stress responses are and how they affect people. She'll find great value in simply knowing that her affliction has a name, that it has physical as well as emotional aspects, and that many other people have suffered from the same syndrome. She will be relieved once she understands the dynamics of normal reaction to extreme stress—denial, disassociation from the trauma, and personality change stemming from attempts to minimize the emotional pain. She'll feel less alone and afraid, her worries about "mental illness" will diminish, and she'll start to regain a feeling of control over her emotions and actions.

For another, the therapist can show her how the traumatic event has damaged her sense of who she is. Little by little, the person with PTSD will be reassured when she learns that many victims feel changed inside after a trauma. She'll be grateful for the knowledge that, with time and personal effort, her own inner "brokenness" can heal.

One of the therapist's most important functions is helping the person with PTSD regain her ability to trust. In successful therapy, the patient first builds a trusting relationship with the therapists; this is called "transference." Then, as she regains feelings of personal competence and control, she's able to branch out. She rebuilds bridges of friendship and support with people she already knows, and she forges links of communication with new people. Eventually she no longer needs the special support of the therapist.

GROUP THERAPY: HEARING OTHER STORIES

One of the valuable extras of hospital-based therapy for PTSD is the opportunity for participation in group therapy. Like other psychiatric problems, PTSD isolates people, making them think they're all alone with their problems. Group therapy gives them the opportunity to learn firsthand that other people are struggling, too. It helps them put their own life in perspective.

You might have imagined that the hospital would have a special therapy group only for PTSD victims, but this isn't so. Therapy groups at the hospital include people with various diagnoses, including depression, anxiety, and alcohol and drug problems. One reason is purely circumstantial: At a given time, there usually aren't enough patients with PTSD to form a separate therapy group. But the other reason is psychological: Meeting people with different problems, seeing how they cope, sharing stories and viewpoints—these are all opportunities to practice open communication. Getting out of the rut of trauma-related thought patterns depends heavily on learning, or relearning, to communicate. Thus, for people overcoming PTSD, group therapy fits nicely into the treatment plan.

Because people with PTSD are so often substance abusers, part of their therapy program may involve another kind of group therapy: attendance at Alcoholics Anonymous (AA) or Narcotics Anonymous (NA) meetings. These 12-step recovery programs have proved helpful to so many patients that quite a few psychiatric hospitals provide space for regular AA and NA meetings. Because these meetings also draw recovering addicts "from the outside," they are a rich source of social contacts. For hospital patients, AA and NA meetings can be an excellent bridge to the larger community.

Trusting, talking, taking part in therapy groups—what's the measure of how well the treatment is working? In other words, what are the signs of recovery from PTSD? That's the next topic for discussion.

Chapter Eleven

Out of the Woods

When someone spends time in treatment for post-traumatic stress disorder, what are the signs of recovery? In other words, when is this person finally out of the woods?

After several weeks or perhaps months of treatment, family members and friends should be able to spot objective evidence of recovery. The individual should seem noticeably *calmer,* more *open* to people and ideas, and *free from alcohol or drug abuse*. Let's consider these criteria one at a time.

CALMING DOWN

As you've learned, part of the definition of PTSD is chronic, inappropriate arousal of the autonomic nervous system. Thus, it's a definite sign of recovery when the person with PTSD begins to seem and act calmer.

Please note that if *panic attacks* have been a problem, it's unrealistic to expect that they will disappear overnight. Most often, overcoming panic attacks is a gradual process. The usual pattern is that after a period of therapy—usually a combination of medication, behavior retraining, and emotional counseling—the person overcoming PTSD reports that her panic attacks seem less severe than before, or are occurring less frequently. As she slowly loses her tendency to have panic attacks, she feels more confident about herself and her ability to face the world.

Or suppose the person with PTSD has a history of *angry outbursts*—flashes of violent temper that frighten the people around him and, in retrospect, frighten him too. When the outbursts stop, or at least diminish in frequency and intensity, that's an indication of recovery in progress. It doesn't mean that the person no longer feels any anger. Rather, it means that psychological counseling is helping him learn how to express anger without losing control. Managing anger constructively is a skill; people who put this skill to work find that it boosts their self-esteem.

Let's say the person with PTSD has been deeply troubled by *instrusive thoughts*. These might be flashbacks—sudden, intense re-experiences of the catastrophe she lived through. Or they might be vivid, frightening fantasies—about committing murder or suicide, for example. Usually intrusive thoughts surface when a particular circumstance, such as being in a crowd, triggers sudden unwanted memories of the traumatic event. If they're severe enough, instrusive thoughts can be obvious to the people around her.

Often, intensive psychotherapy is the most useful approach to subduing intrusive thoughts. As the individual and an emphatic therapist closely re-examine her emotional reaction to the traumatic event, and how it has affected her concept of herself, the unwanted images or fantasies gradually recede. To family and friends, she appears more "together" and in control of herself.

Sleep disturbances are extremely common in PTSD. Sometimes a short course of sleeping medication is part of the therapy. But once again, over the long haul, it's psychotherapy that's most effective at helping the person resolve emotional conflicts that interfere with sleep. When sleep begins to come easily and naturally, that's an indication of recovery from PTSD.

OPENING UP

As you've also learned, PTSD involves not only "hot" symptoms such as panic, anger, intrusive thoughts, and sleep problems, but also "cool" symptoms of detachment. When the "cool" symptoms start to thaw, this too is proof that recovery is under way.

It's likely that *apathy* has been a persistent problem for the person with PTSD. Apathy means a loss of interest in things that used to command his attention and energy: namely, work and recreation. Perhaps he lost his job and made no serious attempt to find another one. Perhaps he stopped seeing his friends. Perhaps he gave up golf or gardening. Psychotherapy will help him redefine what he wants and needs in life, and how he can get it. So when this person begins to emerge from the apathy of PTSD—when he starts a serious job search, or shows renewed interest in seeing people and doing things with them, or picks up his golf clubs or gardening tools again—it's a sign that life again seems worth living. This is an obvious clue that recovery is in process.

Or let's assume for a moment that the person with PTSD suffers from *emotional numbing*. If she isn't feeling anxious or angry, she isn't feeling anything at all; delight, affection, and compassion have disappeared from her emotional repertoire. Emotional numbing stems from defensiveness, which is an attempt to avoid being hurt again. With her therapist, this person will practice evaluating people and events realistically, learning to separate those that are threatening from those that aren't. As she gains skill at this, she will relax her defensive posture. She'll be more open to people and activities that she identifies as potentially enjoyable, and her emotional range will expand. Showing a widened range of emotions is yet another sign of recovery.

A third "cool" symptom of PTSD is *estrangement* from other people. This can mean avoiding family and friends, or feeling unable to deal with any new people, or both. Estrangement involves trauma victims feeling that no one could possibly understand what they lived through, and that since the trauma they are changed, different, "branded" people. A valuable part of therapy for PTSD is education about how people generally respond to severe trauma. When people with PTSD learn that they are not unique—that other people in the world have also experienced profound emotional shock, and have responded much as they did—they gradually begin to feel less isolated and to act less remote and estranged. They renew contact with people who formerly mattered to them and are able to approach and relate to new people. This enhanced sociability is further proof of recovery from PTSD.

LETTING GO OF ALCOHOL AND DRUG DEPENDENCE

Yet another reliable indication of recovery is freedom from alcohol and drug abuse.

As you learned earlier in this book, people with PTSD are extremely prone to alcohol and drug problems. Maybe they drink, smoke marijuana, or live on tranquilizers to calm their raw nerves. Maybe they use cocaine or amphetamines to make up for their lack of energy and motivation. All would be fine if these mood-altering chemicals did their job with no unwanted effects. But the fact is, mood-altering chemicals—also known as "drugs of abuse"—have a bad side as well as a good side. Their bad side is their ability to cause dependence, and eventually addiction.

A person begins drinking or using a drug because it feels good. After a period of time, his *tolerance* for the substance rises. This means he now requires two stiff drinks, instead of just one, to achieve relaxation. Or he now needs Valium every day, instead of once or twice a week, to stay calm. Or he now craves a hit of cocaine or "speed" every afternoon, instead of only on weekends, to feel peppy and alive.

Thus, he increases his consumption. Initially it doesn't seem like a big deal. But by and by, he finds himself trapped into *dependence:* He needs alcohol or drugs all the time to avoid feeling lousy. When he chooses a restaurant or accepts an invitation, he makes sure alcohol will be freely available. When his doctor hesitates to keep renewing the tranquilizer prescription, he angrily switches to a new doctor. When his source of cocaine falters, he's frantic until he secures a new supplier.

At this point, alcohol and drugs have become a major preoccupation. He needs them, in large quantity, just to feel normal. What's more, he's increasingly suffering from physical, mental, and social consequences such as hangovers, tremors, anxiety, memory blackouts, strained personal relationships, frequent accidents, and poor performance on the job. He has slid imperceptibly from dependence into *addiction*. Tragically, the alcohol and drugs that once gave him comfort are now ruining his life.

This slide—from tolerance into dependence and then addiction—is so common among people with PTSD that treatment for substance abuse often plays a major role in their therapy. Hospitalization can be a distinct advantage for such people, because most psychiatric hospitals are well equipped to help people suffering from addictions.

PTSD patients who also suffer from an addiction spend

the first few hospital days in *detoxification*—"going off" alcohol or drugs under medical supervision and with expert nursing support. Then they begin *rehabilitation,* which involves discovering how they slid into addiction, learning how to avoid substance abuse in the future, and building social skills that will help them make their lives satisfying without the aid of mood-altering "crutches." *Group therapy* with other recovering alcohol and drug abusers is always part of the rehabilitation process. Participation in a 12-step *self-help* program, such as Alcoholics Anonymous (AA) or Narcotics Anonymous (NA), is usually required or strongly encouraged.

Thus, the person who gets therapy for PTSD is also likely to be involved in therapy for substance abuse. To this individual's family and friends, his or her ability to give up alcohol and drugs is a major, and very welcome, part of recovery from PTSD.

PERSONAL INTEGRITY

So far, we've been looking at recovery as it appears from the outside. What's more important, although impossible to observe, is the trauma victim's own internal process of recovery. This involves rebuilding a shattered emotional self and recovering a sense of personal integrity. Here are several kinds of learning that take place as a person with PTSD progresses through psychotherapy:

TOLERATING STRONG FEELINGS. Loretta had survived a disastrous hotel fire, partly because she kept her head when others panicked. When she first came to therapy, she was unable to experience strong feelings of any kind—anger, dislike, gratitude, joy—without becoming extremely anxious. She kept her emotional life under wraps by drinking heavily, but she complained of feeling dead inside. As she explored her emotional capacities within the safety of therapy, she was able to "loosen up" and allow herself many feelings she had formerly kept repressed. Bit by bit, she experienced a sense of relief and of inner awakening.

ACCEPTING CONSTRUCTIVE CRITICISM. After surviving an industrial accident, Bob became deeply depressed. He so despised himself that the slightest hint of criticism became a trigger for suicidal feelings. Therapy showed him that he was hypersensitive to criticism because he expected himself to be perfect at all times. As he learned to demand less than total perfection from himself, he also learned how to accept mild, constructive criticism without feeling threatened.

COMFORTING ONESELF. Loretta, the survivor of the hotel fire, discovered during the course of therapy that she walled herself off from emotions to avoid being overwhelmed by anxiety. Part of her therapy was learning how to calm and comfort herself when she felt anxious. She experimented until she found several options that worked for her: giving herself a pep talk while looking in the mirror, unburdening herself to a friend, concentrating on a vigorous exercise workout, or pampering herself with a luxurious hot bath.

APPRECIATING TIME ALONE. At the start of his therapy, Bob, the survivor of the industrial accident, felt panicky whenever he was alone. Unless someone else was right there to reassure him, he felt diminished and somehow unreal, as if perhaps he didn't exist. Cocaine energized him and momentarily filled the void, but it also made him paranoid and "hyper." As Bob recovered from his dependency on cocaine and began to pay attention to his inner needs, he became less frightened of being alone. Eventually he came to enjoy spending a certain amount of time by himself, no longer experiencing aloneness as "loneliness."

INNER STRENGTHS

Another highly personal part of recovering from PTSD is retrieving the inner strengths necessary for coping with life's everyday realities. Ideally, therapy doesn't just replace what was lost, but helps the person grow stronger and more resilient. Here are some examples of the gains in strength that effective therapy can encourage.

SELF-UNDERSTANDING. Carl had stood by helplessly as his best friend Joe died in a barroom brawl-turned-shootout. In the months that followed, Carl became increasingly nervous, jumpy, and depressed. Since he had never spent much time analyzing his feelings, he couldn't tell what was wrong—he just knew the scene of Joe's death was always on his mind. After a number of therapy sessions, he recognized that his feelings about his friend involved not only sadness, but guilt that he hadn't been able to save Joe's life. Working through the guilt helped him regain a sense of self-worth. It also gave him insight into how his feelings could affect his outlook on life. While therapy never did cause Carl to become highly introspective, it did give him some insight into his own reactions and motivations.

RECOGNIZING PERSONAL NEEDS. Linda has always been a people-pleaser. Even when she lost her only son in a tragic accident, she tried to bury her own anguish by concentrating on the physical and emotional needs of her grief-stricken husband and in-laws. She entered therapy because she felt she was having a "nervous breakdown." As she talked with her therapist over a period of weeks, she gradually realized that she had a number of important, unmet psychological needs. Learning how to set personal goals, and work toward reaching them, helped her gratify these needs and let go of her compulsion to minister endlessly to others.

WILLPOWER AND PERSISTENCE. At the start of his

therapy, Carl was so shaken by the violent death of his friend that he was unable to make decisions and stick to them. He had not been a well-organized person to begin with; after the tragedy, in his shock and disorientation, he lapsed into childlike irresponsibility. He made appointments and didn't keep them, got bogged down in simple housekeeping chores, let his bills pile up, and missed days of work without giving notice. Bit by bit, therapy helped Carl put his life in order. As he worked through his grief, he developed a clearer sense of himself and his capabilities. He began to take pleasure in setting priorities and following through on decisions.

AN ENLARGED PERSPECTIVE. All her life Linda had been a dependable helper—slavishly devoted to her family's needs, and lacking any larger outlook. Her personal identity was almost totally submerged; she was hardworking but humorless. In therapy, as she came to terms with her son's tragic death, she developed a new sense of perspective on her own life. For some time, she resented and complained about the heavy demands her family made on her. Later, as she came to see how she herself encouraged her husband and in-laws to be dependent on her, she developed a sense of humor about the situation. The ability to see herself "from the outside," and to laugh at her mistakes, made her psychologically stronger and more self-reliant.

CONCERN FOR OTHERS. People whose world has fallen apart in the wake of a traumatic experience are necessarily self-absorbed. Their energy is scattered; they don't have the time, the concentration, or the self-assurance to think much about other people's feelings. But therapy for PTSD gently brings their energy and attention into focus, allowing them to pay attention to their own needs—and then, eventually, to the needs of others. In people recovering from PTSD, the ability to emphathize with other people's experiences, and to feel concern even for strangers, is proof of growing inner strength.

TRANSFORMATION

Ultimately, the goal of psychotherapy for people with PTSD is to help them *transform* the trauma—a painful, terrifying experience—into a special strength. People who make a full recovery from PTSD may emerge from their experience feeling deeper and wiser. Compared to the way they were before the trauma, they are apt to be more interested in truth, justice, and non-material values. Some feel more spiritual than before. Many find great satisfaction in helping others who are in distress. A sign of transformation might be taking on a leadership role at work or in church, or getting involved in an altruistic community project.

It's unrealistic to expect that *everyone* who recovers from PTSD will become an altruist. For many trauma victims, freedom from the uncomfortable "hot" and "cold" symptoms of PTSD constitutes a perfectly satisfactory recovery. Nevertheless, the full transformation process often does occur—and it's a goal for both the patient and the therapist to keep in mind!

Chapter Twelve

The Walking Wounded

Now that you've seen that therapy for post-traumatic stress disorder can be successful, it's time to consider a sobering question: Do people who have recovered from PTSD live in constant danger of a relapse?

No, not necessarily. It's possible to make a full recovery from PTSD, and go on to lead a satisfying life with no lingering ill effects of past trauma.

But some people who have recovered from PTSD do retain certain emotional vulnerabilities for many years. Whenever life presents them with difficulties they feel they can't handle, there's at least a possibility that some of their old "hot" or "cold" symptoms may reappear.

People with these subtle, lingering vulnerabilities must learn to *recognize* destabilizing events in their lives, and make whatever *changes* are necessary to prevent a relapse of PTSD symptoms. It helps a great deal if family members or close friends understand this and know how to help. What follows is a discussion of some common destabilizing life events, and how to minimize their negative impact on the person who previously suffered from PTSD.

BREAKDOWN OF THE SUPPORT NETWORK

For the survivor of a trauma, as for anyone else, the first line of defense against anxiety is a strong support network. This simply means people—the more, the better—with whom the person shares friendship, help, advice, and social give-and-take. Having a reliable support network keeps the trauma survivor from becoming *isolated*. That's important, because isolation is probably the single factor most likely to lead to a relapse of PTSD symptoms.

Ideally, a support network should include not just family, but outside friends, too. That way, even if family life becomes troubled, the person is not left to cope with these problems in total solitude.

Here's a brief case history to illustrate the point: A woman named Camille, who had been assaulted, beaten, and robbed in a parking lot, suffered from classic PTSD symptoms including chronic anxiety, vivid intrusive images of herself murdering her attackers, and disturbing memory lapses. She sought professional help, and her symptoms gradually subsided. Several years later, Camille's husband moved out of the house and filed for a divorce. Although Camille outwardly seemed to take her husband's desertion with calm and detachment, inside she was angry, bitter, and afraid. Within a few weeks after he left, she began to reexperience some of the same fears and anxieties that had plagued her immediately after the rape. She became tense, fearful, and reclusive. She began to hurry home right after work every day, barricade herself into the house, and take the phone off the hook. She stopped seeing friends. Before long she was severely depressed. It took several months of intensive psychiatric treatment to return her to a precarious normalcy.

As she continued with psychotherapy, Camille came to see that her support network had started to break down when her husband left her—and that she had compounded the problem by isolating herself from other people. She saw that she had leaned heavily on her husband for a sense of identity, and that when he left she felt she no longer existed as a person. With her confidence shaken and her self-image damaged, she fell prey to her old, trauma-related fears.

At the therapist's encouragement, Camille began expanding her support network. She called on old friends. She signed up for a pottery class. She began participating in day excursions organized by the local adult school. A few months later, she acknowledged to the therapist that the added social and intellectual stimulation made her feel more alive and confident. Even though she was still coping daily with the legal and emotional difficulties of divorce, she now had people she could talk to and activities that interested her. Her deep depression had definitely lifted. Although she still felt emotionally fragile, she was no longer haunted by symptoms of PTSD.

Camille's experience illustrates how important it is for the person who has recovered from PTSD to maintain an extensive support network that includes outsiders as well as family members. The misfortune that triggered Camille's relapse of PTSD symptoms was divorce—but divorce isn't the only possible strain on family life. Here are a few other common scenarios in which the family support system breaks down:

- A spouse, child, or parent may die, causing the surviving family members to turn away from each other into private shells of grief.
- Someone in the family may contract a chronic illness, causing the family dynamics to change so that everyone focuses exclusively and obsessively on the sick person.
- Grown children may go off and start their own lives. Parents have to cope, as best they can, with the empty-nest syndrome.

In any of these instances of radical change, "unacceptable" feelings, such as guilt and resentment, may simmer beneath the surface of family life. This is unsettling and frightening—and it may be enough to cause PTSD symptoms to recur.

Those who are close to the person who has recovered from PTSD can help out by encouraging him to have outside-the-family friends. If he has a history of alcohol or drug problems, they can help him keep active in a 12-step program such as Alcoholics Anonymous; regular attendance at AA meetings can provide a very satisfactory circle of sympathetic friends. Involvement in church or synagogue-based volunteer activities is also an excellent way for him to maintain his support network. Membership in an activity-focused organization, such as a book group or a hiking club, also works well.

JOB LOSS

Loss of a job is a seriously destabilizing event that may be particularly hard on the person who has recovered from PTSD. For most people in American society, paid work is the main route to self-esteem. When a former PTSD patient finds herself suddenly jobless, the financial hardship, plus the inevitable drop in self-esteem, may trigger symptoms she thought she had permanently left behind. Self-doubt may cause her to become nervous, jumpy, and anxious. Depression may make her incapable of carrying out an efficient search for a new job. She may begin to experience flashbacks to her traumatic experience, or panic attacks, or sudden unaccountable bursts of furious, destructive anger.

Those close to her can help in several ways. If they see ahead of time that her job is threatened, they can gently help her face this reality, and help her search for a new job "before the axe falls." If she has already lost her job, they can help her think clearly about ways to find new work. Most important, they can simply be there for her, offering a sympathetic ear. As with family turmoil, job loss is a situation where having supportive friends eases the emotional impact of the misfortune and makes a relapse of PTSD symptoms less likely to occur.

ALCOHOL AND DRUG ABUSE

As you've learned, alcohol and drug problems are very often part of PTSD itself, and overcoming dependence or addiction is one of the "musts" of recovery from PTSD. It sometimes happens that a former PTSD patient, who has been sober for many years following recovery from PTSD, starts drinking heavily or using drugs again. The cause is usually an emotional upset—a breakup with a lover, the death of someone close, the collapse of an important business deal, or some other misfortune. Drinking or taking drugs to assuage emotional pain, which is called self-medication, is understandable enough, but it's ultimately destructive, particularly in a person who has previously suffered from addictive illness. Typically, the drinking or drug use progresses from occasional to frequent. If it goes on to become compulsive, the person winds up back where he started, in need of detoxification and rehabilitation.

Those close to the former PTSD patient can help best by *refusing* to play the role of the *enabler*—in other words, by refusing to tolerate or encourage this person's drinking and drug-taking. That sounds simple, but it can be quite tricky. Family members who pour liquor down the drain, or flush away supplies of illegal drugs, will only infuriate the user. Friends who look the other way when their buddy is drunk will only convince him that he isn't really drunk.

Breaking ingrained enabling habits is hard but necessary.

The spouse and children of an alcohol or drug abuser can take a stand by no longer buying alcohol for either him or themselves. They can stop drinking entirely, setting an example of sobriety. They can tell him, gently, that they are concerned about his alcohol or drug consumption. They can stop covering up for blunders and messes he made while drunk or stoned.

Friends can stop enabling, too. They can offer coffee or soda instead of beer or a joint. They can point out to him, gently, that he was "really zonked" at the party the other night. Like family members, friends can tell him they're concerned about his drinking or drug use.

No one can force a person into sobriety, but friends and family members can make life uncomfortable for the alcohol or drug abuser. That's only a first step—but if it prompts the abuser to seek help, or to start going to 12-step recovery meetings again, it may be enough.

EPISODE OF MAJOR DEPRESSION

The last of the common destabilizing events I want to mention is *major depression*. It's important to realize that, while personal setbacks can trigger depression, sometimes depression develops without any perceivable cause.

In so-called endogenous (spontaneous) major depression, a person who has been functioning normally suddenly, and for no apparent reason, begins to feel that everyday life is just too much to handle. Over a period of days, she loses her zest for living. As time goes on, she begins to have sleep and appetite disturbances. She has trouble concentrating, and can't perform her work normally because she gets distracted so often. She feels that she has fallen into a psychological pit, and is completely helpless to pull herself out again. She may seriously contemplate, and even attempt, suicide.

If she formerly suffered from PTSD, this episode of major depression will very likely involve a recurrence of some of the "cool" symptoms of PTSD—a feeling of being cut off and remote, a lack of interest in other people, and emotional and social withdrawal.

The person with endogenous major depression may not even realize that the problem lies within herself. Or, even if she does realize that she is depressed, she may not have the energy necessary to go for professional help. Yet prolonged suffering is needless. With the wide variety of effective medical treatments that are now available, there is no need for her to spend long, agonizing months "riding out" her depression. Some modern forms of treatment for depression start to take effect within days.

When someone who has recovered from PTSD has the misfortune to be overtaken by major depression, a concerned relative or friend can be of great assistance—first, by recognizing that something is wrong, and second, by enabling her to get help for her depression. The help must be very concrete and practical: making the appointment, helping her get ready, driving her there, taking her home afterwards, picking up any prescribed medication she may need, ensuring that she takes her medication as directed, and helping her keep subsequent appointments. Initially, she will be too depressed to show much appreciation. Later on, though, as she gets better, she will be grateful for the help she has received.

EPILOGUE

Fortunately, not everyone who lives through a traumatic event goes on to suffer from post-traumatic stress disorder. Many do, however, and it's for them—and their relatives and friends—that I've written this book.

Symptoms of PTSD are wide-ranging; no two patients, even if they were involved in the same trauma, will have identical reactions. When it comes to therapy, however, certain guiding principles apply to all patients. Thus, in the psychological aftermath of any traumatic event, the key points to keep in mind are these:

- *Counseling right after the trauma may avert the development of PTSD later.*

  It's far better to go overboard, offering debriefing and counseling to *all* survivors of a disaster, than to wait around and see what happens. The chance to review the traumatic event in detail, with a trained counselor, may go a long way toward defusing a potentially explosive buildup of negative emotions.
- *An essential part of therapy for trauma survivors is remembering the trauma in great detail.*

It's easiest for the survivor to remember all the details immediately after the traumatic event. This is another reason why it's better to offer counseling right away, instead of waiting for weeks or months.

- *In psychotherapy for people suffering from PTSD, the true work is making sense of the memories.*

  Simply calling up traumatic memories is only the beginning of therapy. The real work is integrating those memories into the victim's sense of himself, who he is, and what his capabilities and limitations are. This is not an overnight process. It takes time.
- *Once trauma victims achieve a level of trust with their therapist, they're ready to learn to trust others.* When the person suffering from PTSD starts to regain some feeling of personal strength and optimism, she may initially trust no one but her therapist. This reaction, which is called "transference," is quite common; it's a normal step toward recovery. The next step is to help the patient expand her ability to trust, so that she can have meaningful relationships with other people besides the therapist. Her ultimate goal is to recapture, and perhaps surpass, her original pre-trauma level of personal strength and independence.
- *Medication may play a role in therapy for PTSD, but it is never sufficient by itself.* That's because a traumatic experience is an assault on the victim's personal integrity, which has to do with how she experiences herself in the world. Medication can soothe raw nerves temporarily, but its role is merely to set the stage. What happens next—working through feelings of grief and helplessness—is the part of therapy that will have lasting effects.
- *Overcoming alcohol or drug abuse is often a component of therapy for PTSD.* Self-medication with alcohol, prescription pills, or street drugs is a common way for trauma victims to cope with their emotional confusion. But self-

medication often leads to drug dependence, which compounds the person's medical, psychological, and social problems. That's why, for so many PTSD patients, overcoming alcohol and drug abuse is central to effective therapy.

- *Maintaining a strong support network helps keep the former PTSD patient from having a relapse of symptoms.* Isolation is the factor most likely to lead to a recurrence of PTSD symptoms. The best defense is having a variety of regular social contacts—friends as well as family members—with whom to share experiences and feelings.
- *Some PTSD patients are able to "transform" their trauma.* The ultimate goal of PTSD therapy is to turn weakness into strength. When victims have completely integrated their traumatic experience into their personality, their increased self-understanding makes them more understanding of, and more open to, other people. Former PTSD patients who reach this stage may find satisfaction and fulfillment in the helping role, reaching out to those who are disabled or disadvantaged. As a therapist, I have found that this is the most heartwarming result of working with trauma survivors: seeing the phoenix of hope arise from the ashes of misfortune.

Sources

Borton, Lady, "Ambushed by Memory, We Seek Refuge, in Vain," *New York Times*, January 8, 1988, p.C-2.

Bower, B., "Emotional Trauma Haunts Korean POWs," *Science News*, vol.139, February 2, 1991.

———, "Trauma Disorder Strikes Many Young Adults," *Science News*, 139:13 (March 30, 1991), p.198.

Brom, Daniel, et al., "Brief Psychotherapy for Posttraumatic Stress Disorders," *Journal of Consulting and Clinical Psychology*, 57:5 (1989), pp.607–12.

Burstein, Allan, "Treatment Length in Post-Traumatic Stress Disorder," *Psychosomatics*, 27:9 (September 1986), pp.632–37.

———, "Treatment Noncompliance in Patients with Post-Traumatic Stress Disorder," *Psychosomatics*, 27:1 (January 1986), pp.37–40.

Cobb, Steven Michael, "Understanding Psychodynamic Concepts Through Personal Trauma," *Journal of Counseling and Development*, vol.67 (October 1988), p.126.

Coons, Philip M., and Milstein, Victor, "Rape and Post-Traumatic Stress in Multiple Personality," *Psychological Reports*, vol.55 (1984), pp.839–45.

Creamer, Mark, "Post-Traumatic Stress Disorder: Some Diagnostic and Clinical Issues," *Australian and New Zealand Journal of Psychiatry,* 24:517–22 (1990).

Cutler, Blayne, "Enlightened Orphans," *American Demographics,* March 1990, p.16.

Daly, R.J., "Samuel Pepys and Post-Traumatic Stress Disorder," *British Journal of Psychiatry,* 143:64–68 (1983).

Davidson, Jonathan, "Personality in Chronic Post-Traumatic Stress Disorder," *Journal of Anxiety Disorders,* vol.1 (1987), pp. 295–300.

Dicks, Shirley, *From Vietnam to Hell.* Jefferson, N.C. and London: McFarland & Company, 1990.

Dodge, Kenneth, et al., "Mechanisms in the Cycle of Violence," *Science,* vol.250 (December 21, 1990), pp.1678–83.

Dreman, Solly, and Cohen, Esther, "Children of Victims of Terrorism Revisited," *American Journal of Orthopsychiatry,* 60:2 (April 1990), pp.204–209.

Dubrow, Nancy F., and Garbarino, James, "Living in the War Zone: Mothers and Young Children in a Public Housing Development," *Child Welfare,* 68:1 (January/February 1989), pp.3–20.

Eth, Spencer, and Pynoos, Robert S., eds., *Post-Traumatic Stress Disorder in Children.* Washington, D.C.: American Psychiatric Press, 1985.

Figley, Charles R., ed., *Trauma and Its Wake.* New York: Brunner/Mazel, 1985.

Finkelhor, David: "Early and Long-term Effects of Child Sexual Abuse: An Update," *Professional Psychology: Research and Practice,* 21:5 (1990), pp.325–30.

Finney, Angus, "Delayed Effects of Trauma," *New Statesman and Society,* December 23–30, 1988, p.26.

Ford, Charles V., "Post-Traumatic Therapy and Victims of Violence," *New England Journal of Medicine,* August 25, 1988, p.524.

Forrman, Stuart I., and Havas, Stephen, "Massachusetts' Post-Traumatic Stress Disorder Program: A Public Health

Treatment Model for Vietnam Veterans," *Public Health Reports*, 105:2 (March-April 1990), pp. 172–79.

Gould, Mark A., *A Consumer's Guide to Psychiatric Diagnosis*. Summit, N.J.: PIA Press, 1989.

Gross, Jane, "Aftershocks Damaging Frail Psyches," *New York Times*, October 26, 1989, p. B8.

———"Even the Victim Can Be Slow to Recognize Rape," *New York Times*, May 28, 1991, p. A14.

Hamilton, Denise, "Reliving Terror," Los Angeles *Times*, January 28, 1991.

Helzer, John E., et al, "Post-Traumatic Stress Disorder in the General Population," *New England Journal of Medicine*, vol.317 (December 24, 1987), pp.1630–34.

Hoffman, LInda, et al., "Low Plasma B-Endorphin in Post-Traumatic Stress Disorder," *Australian and New Zealand Journal of Psychiatry*, 29:2 (1989), pp.269–73.

Hryvniak, Michael R., and Rosse, Richard B., "Concurrent Psychiatric Illness in Inpatients with Post-Traumatic Stress Disorder," *Military Medicine*, 154:8 (August 1989), pp.399–401.

Hytten, Karsten, and Herlofsen, Pal, "Accident Simulation as a New Therapy Technique for Post-Traumatic Stress Disorder," *Acta Psychiatrica Scandinavica*, Supplement 355, vol.80 (1989), pp.79–83.

James, Beverly, *Treating Traumatized Children*. Lexington, Mass.: Lexington Books, 1989.

Johnson, Kendall, *Trauma In the Lives of Children*. Claremont, Cal.: Hunter House, 1989.

Jordan, Charles S., "Psychophysiology of Structural Imagery in Post-Traumatic Stress Disorder," *Journal of Mental Imagery*, 8:4 (1984), pp.51–66.

Jordan, Harold W., et al., "Post-Traumatic Stress Disorder: A Psychiatric Defense," *Journal of the National Medical Association*, 78:2 (1986), pp.119–26.

Kohn, Alfie, "Shattered Innocence," *Psychology Today*, February 1987, pp.54–58.

Kolb, Lawrence C., "Chronic Post-Traumatic Stress Disorder: Implications of Recent Epidemiological and Neuropsychological Studies," *Psychological Medicine*, vol.19 (1989), pp.821–24.

Koss, Mary P., "The Women's Mental Health Research Agenda: Violence Against Women," *American Psychologist*, 45:3 (March 1990), pp.374–80.

Kuch, Klaus, et al., "Post-Traumatic Stress Disorder After Car Accidents," *Canadian Journal of Psychiatry*, 30:426-427 (October 1985), p. 426-427.

Kuhne, Arthur, et al., "Completeness and Internal Consistency of *DSM-III-R* Criteria for Post-Traumatic Stress Disorder," *Journal of Clinical Psychology*, 44:5 (September 1988), pp.717–22.

Kutz, Ilan, et al, "Post-Traumatic Stress Disorder Following Myocardial Infarction," *General Hospital Psychiatry*, 10 (1988), p. 169-176.

Lindy, Jacob D., "Transference and Post-Traumatic Stress Disorder," *Journal of the American Academy of Psychoanalysis*, 17:3 (1989), pp.397–413.

Lucking, Robert G., "Bipolar Disorder in Post-Traumatic Stress Disorder—A Difficult Diagnosis: Case Reports," *Military Medicine*, vol.151 (May 1986), pp.282–284.

Matsakis, Aphrodite, *Vietnam Wives*. Rockville, MD: Woodbine House, 1988.

McCann, I. Lisa, and Pearlman, Laurie Anne, *Psychological Trauma and the Adult Survivor*. New York: Brunner/Mazel, 1990.

McFarlane, A.C., "An Australian Disaster: The 1983 Bushfires," *International Journal of Mental Health*, 19:2 (1990), pp.36–47.

Mikulincer, Mario, and Solomon, Zahava, "Attributional Style and Combat-Related Posttraumatic Stress Disorder," *Journal of Abnormal Psychology*, 97:3 (1988), pp.308–13.

Navarro, Mireya, "For Some, No Escape from L.I. Jet Crash," *New York Times*, June 25, 1990, p. B1.

Ochberg, Frank M., ed., *Post-Traumatic Therapy and Victims of Violence*. New York: Brunner/Mazel, 1988.

O'Connor, Colleen, with Doherty, Shawn, "A Vietnam Vet's Suicide Pact," *Newsweek*, March 17, 1986, p. 30.

Patten, Sylvia, et al., "Post-Traumatic Stress Disorder and the Treatment of Sexual Abuse," *Social Work*, May 1989, pp.197–203.

Peebles, Mary Jo, "Through a Glass Darkly: The Psychoanalytic Use of Hypnosis with Post-Traumatic Stress Disorder," *International Journal of Clinical and Experimental Hypnosis*, 37:3 (1989), pp.192–206.

Pitman, Roger K., "Post-Traumatic Stress Disorder, Conditioning, and Network Theory," *Psychiatric Annals*, 18:3 (March 1988), pp.182–89.

———, "Post-Traumatic Stress Disorder, Hormones, and Memory," *Biological Psychiatry*, 26:221–23 (1989).

Quen, Jacques M., ed., *Split Minds/Split Brains*. New York and London: New York University Press, 1986.

Raymond, Chris Anne, "Study Says Memories of Violent Death Linger in Survivors, Trigger Psycosocial Problems," *JAMA* 259:24, p. 3524.

Resick, Patricia A., "Post-Traumatic Stress Disorder in a Vietnam Nurse: Behavioral Analysis of a Case Study," *Women and Therapy*, 5:1 (Spring 1986), pp.55–65.

Rothblum, Esther D., and Cole, Ellen, eds., *A Woman's Recovery From the Trauma of War*. New York: Haworth Press, 1986.

Sack, David A., *No More Secrets, No More Shame*. Summit, N.J.: PIA Press, 1990.

Saigh, Philip A., "Anxiety, Depression, and Assertion Across Alternating Intervals of Stress," *Journal of Abnormal Psychology*, 97:3 (1988), pp.338–431.

Sandrick, Karen, "Expanded Delivery System Needed for Post-Traumatic Stress," *Hospitals*, June 5, 1990, pp.44–45.

Shapiro, Francine, "Eye Movement Desensitization: A New

Treatment for Post-Traumatic Stress Disorder," *Journal of Behavioral Therapy and Experimental Psychiatry,* 20:3 (1989), pp.211–17.

Shehan, Constance L., "Spouse Support and Vietnam Veterans' Adjustment to Post-Traumatic Stress Disorder," *Family Relations,* vol.36 (January 1987), pp.55–60.

Shephard, Ben, "Vietnam 'vets;' and the Soviet experience," *History Today,* vol.39 (July 1989), pp.10–12.

Shore, James H., *Disaster Stress Studies: New Methods and Findings.* Washington, D.C.: American Psychiatric Press, 1986.

Shroyer, Jo Ann, "Becoming Streetwise: Guidelines for Female Runners," *The Physician and Sportsmedicine,* 18:2 (February 1990), pp.121–25.

Slaby, Andrew E., *Aftershock.* New York: Villard, 1989.

Slagle, Dodge A., et al., "Community Psychological Effects Following a Non-fatal Aircraft Accident," *Aviation, Space, and Environmental Medicine,* 61:10 (October 1990), pp.879–86.

Spiegel, David, "Multiple Personality as a Post-Traumatic Stress Disorder," *Psychiatric Clinics of North America,* 7:1 (March 1984), pp.101–110.

Stern, Theodore A., "Helping Your Patient Recover from Disaster," *Medical Economics,* May 21, 1990, pp.162–72.

Sutker, Patricia B., et al., "Trauma-Induced Weight Loss and Cognitive Deficits Among Former Prisoners of War," *Journal of Consulting and Clinical Psychology,* 58:3 (1990), pp.323-28.

Taylor, A.J.W., *Disasters and Disaster Stress.* New York: AMS Press, 1989.

Thompson, Rosemary A., "Strategies for Crisis Management in the Schools," *NAASP Bulletin,* February 1990, pp.54–58.

Ulman, Richard B., and Brothers, Doris, *The Shattered Self.* Hillsdale, N.J.: The Analytic Press, 1988.

van der Kolk, Bessel A., "The Drug Treatment of Post-Traumatic Stress Disorder," *Journal of Affective Disorders,* vol.13 (1987), pp.203–13.

Watson, Charles G., et al., "The Relationships of Post-Traumatic Stress Disorder to Adolescent Illegal Activities, Drinking, and Employment," *Journal of Clinical Psychology,* 44:4 (July 1988), pp.592–98.

Watson, I.P. Burges, et al., "The Neuropsychiatry of Post-Traumatic Stress Disorder," *British Journal of Psychiatry,* vol.152 (1988), pp.164–73.

Wilson, John P., *Trauma, Transformation, and Healing*. New York: Brunner/Mazel, 1989.

Wolf, Marion E. and Mosnaim, Aron D., eds., *Posttraumatic Stress Disorders*. Washington, D.C.: American Psychiatric Press, 1990.

Index

ABOUT THE AUTHOR

HAROLD A. LEVINE, D.O., is a practicing psychiatrist with extensive experience in the academic community and in private practice. He is the Medical Director at Oak Creek Hospital in San Jose, California. Following his residency and fellowship training in adult and adolescent psychiatry at the Menninger Foundation in Topeka, Kansas, Dr. Levine served as an Assistant Professor of Psychiatry at the University of Health Sciences in Kansas City, Missouri. Dr. Levine has also served as the Medical Director of various psychiatric hospitals in Arizona and California. Dr. Levine is a member of the American Psychiatric Association and is Board Certified in Adult Psychiatry.